Disarming the Heart

Toward a Vow of Nonviolence

John Dear

Paulist Press
New York/Mahwah

Library of Congress Cataloging-in-Publication Data

Dear, John, 1959–
    Disarming the heart.

    Bibliography: p.
    1. Nonviolence—Religious aspects—Christianity. 2. Dear, John,
1959–   . I. Title.
BT736.6.D42   1986   241'.69   86-18697
ISBN 0-8091-2842-X (pbk.)

Published by Paulist Press
997 Macarthur Boulevard
Mahwah, New Jersey 07430

Printed and bound in the United States of America

Contents

Acknowledgments

I would like to express my gratitude to Frank McAloon, Peter Cicchino, and Edward Thomas, good friends and brothers, who shared with me the grace of vowing nonviolence.

I also want to express my appreciation to my friends who gave me many good suggestions and much encouragement with these reflections: Bill Sneck who helped me along from the beginning, Peter Cicchino, Monika Hellwig, Jack Marth, Eileen Egan, Mary Lou Kownacki, Harry Geib, Joe Sands, Charlie McCarthy, Donald Campion, Ed DeBerri, and Mary Evelyn Jegen. Thanks, too, for the witness and faith of my friends and co-workers in Central America.

I would also like to thank Richard McSorley and Daniel Berrigan for teaching me by word and example what the goods news is all about.

May the Lord of peace and love bring us all into that kingdom where there is no fear and no violence.

The way of peace is the way of truth ... Truthfulness is even more important than peacefulness. Indeed, lying is the mother of violence. A truthful person cannot long remain violent. He will perceive in the course of his research that he has no need to be violent, and he will further discover that so long as there is the slightest trace of violence in him, he will fail to find the truth he is searching for.

Mohandas Gandhi

The choice today is no longer between violence and non-violence. It is either nonviolence or nonexistence.

Martin Luther King, Jr.

Preface

A group of political activists were attempting to show the Master how their ideology would change the world.

The Master listened carefully.

The following day he said, "An ideology is as good or bad as the people who make use of it. If a million wolves were to organize for justice, would they cease to be a million wolves?"

Might this be the problem facing the peace movement today? Perhaps nothing changes because under the sheeps' clothing rest wolves—a million or more wolves fighting for a freeze, battling for a ban on nuclear testing, sparring for an end to star wars.

And wolves—every child knows—are not instruments of peace; wolves are wagers of war.

It is the most ancient of axioms that John Dear's book addresses: to have peace in our world we must first have peace within ourselves. We cannot have peace with hate in our hearts. The method that John suggests for disarming the heart is a vow of nonviolence.

A couple of years ago I struggled to face the demons within by taking a vow of nonviolence in the middle of a desert. Taking any vow in any desert would be terrifying enough—all is stripped to zero—but to proclaim the non-violent message of Jesus in this desert was to put the pow-

ers of darkness to severe test. In this Nevada desert lurked
the demon named legion. Here all United States nuclear
test explosions occurred, an announced test taking place
every three weeks. On the fortieth anniversary of the bomb-
ing of Hiroshima, a small group had gathered in this desert
to commit civil disobedience and call for an end to nuclear
weapons testing.

Prior to the action, two of us recited a vow of nonviolence—a simple "no" to death. Yet, one felt the tremors
beneath the scorching sands, the gods of war thrashing
wildly in sleep, nightmares beyond imagining, their restless
sleep the result of similar actions occurring simultaneously
in the nation. At the invitation of Pax Christi USA, Christians across the country were signaling a total break with
violence by reciting a simple vow of nonviolence.

Each day the numbers grow. In cities and small towns
everywhere, people from all walks of life, are promising:
"Recognizing the violence in my own heart, yet trusting in
the goodness and mercy of God, I vow for one year to practice the nonviolence of Jesus. . . ."

In unknown places like Bonaire, Georgia, and Poplar-
ville, Mississippi, small cells of peacemakers are meeting
and praying over the vow of nonviolence. Some decide to
ritualize the vow. In Sarasota, Florida, seven took the vow
at a weekday Mass, one being a seventy-five year old
woman, blind from birth, her copy of the vow written in
braille. In Seattle, Washington, Maxyne McCall took her
vow with thirty supportive friends and the blessing of Arch-
bishop Raymond Hunthausen. After the ceremony, as a
sign of community with each other and all peoples of the
world, the group enjoyed a meal with dishes from seven
war-torn nations. In California, Bishop Francis A. Quinn
traveled one hundred and eighty miles to witness a small

vow ceremony; in Waterville, Massachusetts, Bishop Amedee W. Proulx presided at a service where fifty people pledged nonviolence.

Priests are weaving the vow into their ordination masses; sisters into their profession ceremonies; both into their jubilee celebrations.

Some are taking the vow alone, in the privacy of a retreat center or their own homes. "On this cold day in April, sitting alone in my room, I wish to make my vow of nonviolence," wrote Hazel L. Ordway, of Piscataway, New Jersey. "I have been to Mass and have read the morning prayers of the Office. . . . I shall write down the vow I'm sending you, trusting that by doing so it may be etched permanently in my mind and heart."

There are more dramatic settings. Paul Magno, one of the Plowshares resisters, took the vow while in a federal prison. A Jesuit scholastic in El Salvador knelt before the tomb of Oscar Romero and recited the vow of nonviolence, then continued on his way to Chile to serve the poor.

But it's in the letters that pour into the national office of Pax Christi USA that the inner revolution to transform the wolf is revealed.

"In Nicaragua, where over half the population is fifteen years of age or younger, the cry of the poor is especially the cry of children," wrote Len Calabrese of Cleveland. "I can't forget the cries of two year old Norma Elena Chavarria, whose tiny malnourished body and seeping sores became a living symbol for me of the indescribable horrors caused by generations of violence, much of it coming from North America. Washing Norma Elena in the Paiwas River had a powerful effect on me, as did putting ointment on her sores. It was as if I were baptized in the healing waters of forgiveness and anointed for the path of nonviolence.

Somehow, a profound letting go took place. The vow is a way of continuing that letting go."

Rev. Doug Doussan, national chairperson of Pax Christi, made this observation: "Many of us who took the vow of nonviolence last year made a frightening discovery in preparing for that important event. While calling for nonviolent solutions to international conflicts and an end to all weapons of violence, we discovered that violence had set up a comfortable home in our hearts.

"The words of St. Francis of Assisi became an indictment: 'While you are proclaiming peace with your lips, be careful to have it even more fully in your heart.' Taking the vow became not so much a witness to an already achieved stance and style of life but a new beginning of a more serious effort toward a 'consistent life ethic' of nonviolence."

Those striving for a "consistent life ethic" of nonviolence will find in this book both the rationale for a vow of nonviolence and reflections on its implications.

John himself is the model of a process still in embryo, but possessed with a potential to birth a peace church. A young man hears the call to take a vow of nonviolence. After reflection and prayer, he takes the step in total darkness, trusting without reservation, even though it leads him to places where he would rather not go. Faithfully he begins to record his experiments in unconditional love, the first fruit being this book.

Now imagine all those who have taken the vow of nonviolence doing similar experimenting and reflection. Eventually a theology of peace, rooted in the lived experience of the faithful, begins to emerge, a theology of peace that fearlessly faces those tenets of Jesus now largely ignored in Christian life: unlimited forgiveness, love of enemies, Christ's reconciliation through suffering and death, rejection of violence.

Can we imagine such a church? That depends. Can we imagine a million or more lambs organizing for peace?

Mary Lou Kownacki, O.S.B.
National Coordinator
Pax Christi USA

Foreword

$\mathbf{N}$othing could be more urgent in our world today than work for peace and genuine community among the peoples and races of mankind. Under the threat of nuclear war and of nuclear accidents, more and more people are coming to realize this and to be constantly preoccupied with the fear of violence on an unprecedented scale. Yet most feel quite powerless to do anything about it.

Peace has always been identified with biblical and Christian hope. Indeed it has been seen as the condition of God's reign among human people, and therefore as the condition of salvation and the work of redemption. What Christians knew so clearly at the beginning has sometimes faded with increase in numbers, wider dispersion over the face of the earth, and more complex responsibilities and relationships. The earliest followers of Jesus realized all too clearly that peace and community spread from the heart outward into social structures of groups and peoples, from the grass roots experiences and relationships of individuals into the higher echelons of social control. Those earliest Christians set out to be leaven in the world. They did not seek to dominate but to permeate. And in large measure they were successful.

The history of our betrayal of these ideals through the centuries has been documented many times. What is really far more important is to set about recapturing the spirit and

1

the strategy of radical peace-making and radical community building. The latter has been the focus of attention for some time, especially in third world countries, in the formation of basic Christian communities, raising a newly revitalized consciousness of what it means to be Church, to be people of God, to be members one of another. But there is need also to pursue the Christian task of peace-making directly, indeed to reflect deeply on a continuing *praxis* of peace-making by people seriously and deliberately committed to this as Christians.

It is in this context that the vow of non-violence is an idea whose time has most definitely come in our own days. The spontaneity with which many different types of people, many different groups, have embraced the idea and sought formulations by which to express and pursue it together shows how opportune such a vow is to our times. Known in biblical language by the less popular term of "meekness," the idea of non-violence as an evangelical counsel is certainly not new. Nor is the idea of committing oneself by vow to the fulfilling of a particular counsel of perfection a new one. Yet for historical reasons we have tended to isolate the vows of poverty, chastity and obedience as the classical expression of the commitment to follow evangelical counsels of perfection. It is historical reasons again which so urgently suggest the inadequacy of an exclusive promotion of these three vows in our times.

John Dear does a signal service to the Church of our times in setting before us a book in which he traces the meaning, the manner of implementation and the models that may be followed for a vow of non-violence in our times. It is a book that will be helpful to those who already share John Dear's own deep commitment to a life of creative and searching Christian non-violence. It will be an immense encouragement and inspiration to those who wish they shared that commitment and would like to move a little closer, and it will be a challenge not easily ignored by those who read the book out of curiosity or by the importunity of their friends. May it fall into many hands and breed peace!

Monika K. Hellwig

A Vow of Nonviolence

Recognizing the violence in my own heart, yet trusting in the goodness and mercy of God, I vow to practice the nonviolence of Jesus who taught us in the Sermon on the Mount:

> Blessed are the peacemakers, for they shall be called sons and daughters of God. . . . You have learned how it was said, "You must love your neighbor and hate your enemy"; but I say to you, "Love your enemies, and pray for those who persecute you. In this way, you will be sons and daughters of your Father in heaven."

Before God the Creator and the Sanctifying Spirit, I vow to carry out in my life the love and example of Jesus by striving for peace within myself and seeking to be a peacemaker in my daily life; by accepting suffering rather than inflicting it; by refusing to retaliate in the face of provocation and violence; by persevering in nonviolence of tongue and heart; by living conscientiously and simply so that I do not deprive others of the means to live; by actively resisting evil and working nonviolently to abolish war and the causes of war from my own heart and from the face of the earth.

God, I trust in your sustaining love and believe that just as you gave me the grace and desire to offer this, so you will also bestow abundant grace to fulfill it.

5

Introduction

It was a hot August morning. Three friends and I climbed up a hill in rural Pennsylvania and sat down in a shady place between four giant pine trees. There was a great excitement in the air. We began to sing and our celebration began. After long anticipation and much preparation, we were about to profess perpetual vows of nonviolence.

We read the two great commandments to love God and neighbor, and then prayed: "Almighty and eternal God, to you all hearts are open, all desires known, and from you no secrets are hid. Cleanse the thoughts of our hearts by the inspiration of your Holy Spirit, that we may perfectly love you, and worthily magnify your holy name; through Christ. Amen."

Then, we took turns confessing—openly and honestly—our sins and our use of violence. After this act of contrition, a great stillness and calm came upon us. The Spirit of forgiveness was poured out on each of us in a very personal way as we took turns laying hands on each other and praying for each other silently. We then signed our forgiveness and reconciliation by embracing one another.

We recited psalms and scriptural readings, including a passage from the Sermon on the Mount: "Love your enemies, do good to those who hate you, bless those who curse you, pray for those who treat you badly. . . . Do good and lend without any hope of return. Be compassionate. . . . Do not judge. . . . Do not condemn. . . . Grant pardon . . ." (Lk 6:27–38).

We each then reflected on our commitment to the way of nonviolence and how we had come to that moment, to professing a vow of nonviolence. We spoke of the difficulties and risks that it would involve, the great freedom that it would give to us, and the solidarity with the poor, the humility and prayer needed to be faithful to God through the grace of the vow. We shared our thoughts about the need to be actively involved in fighting injustice and violence through nonviolence and love for the rest of our lives. We shared our commitment to each other to support one another in the vow, and our joy and consolation in knowing that nonviolence is an answer to the world's age-old questions about life and meaning. Our reflection reinforced one simple conclusion: "Nonviolence is for us a way to God, to love, to Truth."

Then, before a simple wooden cross, we each professed the following vow (which we wrote according to the tradition of our community): "Almighty and eternal God, Father of Jesus and Mother of all creation, you worked the salvation of the world through the life and death of your Son and the outpouring of the Spirit. In his perfect act of suffering, nonviolent love, Jesus gave his life as a ransom for the many, and redeemed his lost sisters and brothers from sin. Trusting in your infinite goodness and mercy, I, before the cross of Jesus Christ, vow perpetual nonviolence in fulfillment of the command of your Son and in imitation of his holy life and death. I seek the intercession of the Blessed Virgin Mary and all your saints. Father, I trust in your sustaining love and believe that just as you gave me the grace to desire and offer this, so you will also bestow abundant grace to fulfill it."

As we witnessed each other make the promise, our hearts were filled with joy and consolation, with the great love of God. Our response was a joyous exultation of God, the Magnificat of Mary (Lk 1:46–55).

We prayed for peace in the world, for the poor and the oppressed, for the end of injustice and the coming of God's kingdom. We offered the Lord's Prayer and closed with the plea: "God of perfect peace, violence and cruelty can have no part with you. May those who are at peace with one another hold fast to the good will that unites them; may those who are enemies forget their hatred and be healed." After a final blessing and praise, we broke into joyful song.

For the four of us, this vow of nonviolence was a powerful, personal experience of the love of God. We knew that we were embarking on a new course, opening a new door into the unknown realm of God's grace which would call us to be faithful to such a vow and to accept its consequences. Yet, we had not anticipated that the profession of our vow of nonviolence itself would prove to be such a beautiful gift from God. Our response was gratitude and praise. We realized that we had been missioned then and there to be and to become instruments of God's nonviolence. It was a beautiful beginning to our new lives.

I had come to that moment after a year and a half of consideration, contemplation, discussion and experimentation in nonviolence. I first began to consider professing a vow of nonviolence while making the thirty day silent retreat of St. Ignatius Loyola, the Spiritual Exercises. Deep reflection on the Gospel of Jesus and how I could further accept God's disarming love brought me to realize that love is not compatible with violence in thought, word or deed.

During the Spiritual Exercises, I decided I would spend some time studying nonviolence and continue praying for the grace to know how God is calling me to be a follower of Jesus, a peacemaker. I spent over a year and a half considering the commitment and the call of vowed nonviolence, discussing it with my friends, experimenting with it and studying the lives and writings of the great practitioners of Gospel nonviolence. This period of prayer, discussion, consideration and study, intermingled with service to the poor and the building of community, led me to want to accept God's disarming love wholeheartedly and to live that love with all my life.

Since that time, the vow has been a channel of grace for me in my life and work for peace and justice in Washington, D.C. and in New York City, in many experiments of nonviolent love at military installations and federal buildings, in marches, public acts of civil disobedience and vigils. It has also been a channel of grace that guided me as I tried to follow the way of Jesus while I was living in El Salvador in a refugee camp and visiting other places in Central America.

It is from my own experience of this vow of nonviolence that I write these reflections with the desire to share them with others who may be so moved to profess a similar vow of nonviolence. I simply want to share a way to God which I have found helpful. I write both to those drawn to nonviolence who have not considered a vow, and to those who are unfamiliar with the way of nonviolence.

This is a simple set of reflections that have proved a starting point for me. After briefly reviewing what is meant by the terms "violence" and "nonviolence," there is a general discussion on vows and the vow of nonviolence. After looking at some of the many reasons for professing a vow of nonviolence in our day and age and some of the implications for the life of vowed nonviolence, I touch on some further questions about the very idea of a vow of nonviolence. I conclude with a look at Gandhi, who first professed "a vow of nonviolence," and Jesus, who is, and always will be, the great teacher, exemplar and model of nonviolence.

1

Forgetting Who We Are

We lined up in a long row behind the old blue bus. I stood in the middle of the highway along with fifty or so Salvadoran campesinos who were traveling in El Salvador to the town of Chalatenango. Our bus was stopped and searched by the army. All the women were forced to line up in front of the bus. It was a Sunday afternoon and there was not another sign of life as far as we could see. We were in the middle of barren fields, surrounded by huge mountains far away on the horizon. We were somewhere in the north of El Salvador and we were surrounded by young Salvadoran soldiers with machine guns aimed at us.

It was a normal road check. The soldiers were looking for guerrillas or weapons that were being transported. But there was fear in the air; the weapons were meant to intimidate and to protect. I realized that any kind of accident could happen and I looked to see how the other Salvadorans alongside me were responding. They simply bowed their heads and stood in silence. We were all searched one by one and questioned as to our reasons for traveling in this part of the country. After a while, we were permitted to get back on the bus and we proceeded on our way.

On that day in El Salvador, I saw brothers and sisters acting toward one another as if they were objects or things to be feared or pushed around. I saw children of God sadly

13

trapped into a way of life, dehumanizing one another and themselves.

Violence is best defined as that act of forgetting or ignoring who we are: brothers and sisters of one another, each one of us a child of God. Violence occurs in those moments when we forget and deny our basic identity as God's children, when we treat one another as if we were worthless instead of priceless and cling to our own selfish desires, possessions and security. It can become a trap, a way of life in which we see no way out, in which we find no hope, in which we become unable to look into one another's eyes with love and respect. Violence is any behavior that dehumanizes us, from thoughts of self-hatred to intentional harm or physical injury done to another. Our apathy and indifference in the face of relievable suffering and our willingness to defend our possessions and self-interests have harmful effects on others and are a participation in violence. The lack of love and the anxiety in our hearts, the unwillingness to suffer with others and to forgive others, and the insecurity, the fears and untruth in which we frame our lives are all participations in violence because their consequences are harmful to others.

Violence begins in our hearts when we give in to temptation and become anxious and fearful, when we lose inner peace and harmony. As we forget or ignore the reality that we are all equal, all chidren of a loving God, all brothers and sisters of one another, our hearts turn from truth and love. This negative state of forgetfulness feeds on itself and soon we find ourselves lying, hating and cheating others. Our communication with others is disrupted and we act as if we do not recognize who the other person is or who other people are. Any common ground of equality or understanding vanishes. We become unable to see the world from the perspective of others and we cling to our own absolute idea of right and wrong. In our self-centeredness, we become blind and unconcerned about others, especially those who are suffering.

When we characterize another or others as enemies, when we look with fear and suspicion at others, we reveal the violence in our own hearts, the fact that we have forgotten to whom we are relating. When we respond to threats or acts of violence by using violence or by passively receiving the violence, we act in ways that go against what is good for us, what we would truly desire if we only understood the fact of our common heritage as sons and daughters of God. In the spiral of violence, the perception of another as "enemy" stimulates the use of violence which in turn encourages that other person or group to label the initiators of the violence as "enemy." Charles McCarthy defines an enemy as "one or many who negatively affect the survival of some self-interest," such as life, possessions, reputation or power.[1] An "enemy" poses a threat of harm to oneself, or to one's values, friends or possessions, or may have already committed violence toward oneself or one's self-interest. Quarrels and conflicts begin when opposing people insist and scream at each other: "I'm absolutely right." With this absolute conviction and unwillingness to listen, people feel justified in harming and then killing one another.

Once we forget who we are and begin to act violently, we start to legitimize what we do and to systematize our wickedness. We keep working at this legitimization to defend our perceptions, our use of violence. With the systemic violence of society, we try to encourage one another to accept violence. The way of violence becomes a habit too hard to break. Sometimes we find ourselves in situations where we defend our use of violence and we are unable to break the habit, unable to change, unable to risk another way of life. We adopt patriotic and nationalistic symbols and ideologies which can divide us and we get caught in an uncontrollable, unreflected spirit which separates us and divides us from the whole human family. Soon we lose any faith in God and do not believe in the reality of the human family. Once we find ourselves in such an apparently hopeless situation, we can fall into greater despair, helplessness and self-hatred.

We create idols which take the place of the one true God, since by this time we have lost any sight of God's presence in the other person. Idolatry is our denial of God's existence in others and the placing of our faith and trust in anything or anyone other than God. Our new idols become our only security, our way of defending the forgetfulness, the lie that we are living in and the violence that we do. The nuclear arms race, for example, is the practice of idolatry: people have placed their faith, trust and dependence on nuclear weapons and not in God. We have forgotten that we are one family, have greedily pursued selfish interests, and have produced nuclear weapons to protect our possessions. The end result of this denial of God has been the violence committed against the poor who starve and suffer disease, illiteracy, and homelessness. Wealth, the desire for honor, and pride kill the Spirit in each of us, cause systemic violence against the poor, and lead to new and bigger idolatries in our world, such as the nuclear arms race, consumerism, abortion, sexism and classism.

Charles McCarthy defines violence specifically as "responding to a person as an object for the purpose of self-gratification. Violence is forgetting or ignoring that there is an infinity behind every human face."[2] When we deny the presence of God, of love and truth in another human being, we are committing violence. We are forgetting or ignoring who we are and what we are about. All of us forget who we are at various moments in our lives and so we all commit violence. The struggle of life is not to accept and legitimize our forgetfulness, our violence, but to repent of it and over-come it by doing good, by actively loving others.

When we forget who we are, we commit violence which results in physical injury and death to others, usually the destitute and voiceless poor of the third world. When we commit these acts of violence, when we deviate from love and truth, we do not know what we are doing.

The violence that happens when we forget or ignore our basic identities can take various forms on a continuum of violence, depending on the extent to which we have for-gotten or ignored our basic identity. This spectrum includes any use of emotional, psychological, personal, communal or international manipulation or domination by one's will over and against another's will. Violence can take the form, on one end of the spectrum, of hatred and lying which we hold in our hearts and publicly deny and, on the other end, can include the use of physical force or power to damage or destroy humanity. It can come under the form of a spirit which makes people do what they do not want to do: threaten and inflict physical harm or any other form of punishment on others. Our support of the unjust, judgmen-tal values of society which have led us into a nuclear arms race and militarism, and force the majority of the world into poverty, starvation, disease, homelessness, the denial of human dignity, and other injustices, is a participation in violence and a legitimization of violence. The systematic wickedness of good people in society who use cultural structures such as educational and religious institutions to defend their ideas and possessions, or who continue to work for money-making, military institutions and factories, legitimates violence. Destitution and poverty which result in early and unjust deaths among the world's poor are caused by the greed and selfishness of people who are too afraid to risk a break with the way of violence and who forget or ignore the fact that every participation in so called legitimate, systemic violence has a harmful consequence somewhere down the line on others. Our greed causes direct physical harm and death to the world's poor and thus each large and small act of greed can harm others.

Violence in society and in one's heart is a false peace, an absence of love, life and real truth, and is usually founded on self-hatred, fear and lies. It kills one's soul when it appears to be protecting and saving one's life. Violence is the step toward spiritual death which one takes when one gives in to any suicidal temptation. It is any refusal of God's gift of life. It leads not only to the death of others, but to the fulfillment of one's own suicidal spirit.

This state of violence is a state of nothingness and meaninglessness, a denial of our identities and our existence as loved children of God, where each one of us is equal and precious in God's sight. In violence, we forget our God and act as if we have no God. When we reject love, truth, hope and God in our everyday choices, in our complicity, apathy, boredom and passivity, and in the bigger decisions of our values, employment, and lifestyles, we reject ourselves and the life we can lead as children of God. Throughout history, violence has continued to lead to nothing but unhappiness, meaninglessness, despair, hunger, war, suicide, the creation and use of nuclear weapons, the perpetuation of unjust social systems, and more violence.

The struggle to be human in today's world involves overcoming the forces of violence which attack everyone from every side. In the effort to claim our inheritance as loved children of God, we must claim our love for one another and *choose life*. We must *remember* who we are.

We must recall and return to the knowledge and awareness of our identity. We do not want to forget. We do not mean to do violence. But we do forget, each one of us. Nonviolence is a way of remembering and recalling, every day of our lives, who we are and what we are about, and returning to that life whenever we forget. It is noncooperation with violence, a refusing to forget. Nonviolence is a way out of the trap of violence. Nonviolence offers a way toward the fuller life of love and community as God's children. It is a way that can help us to be one human family, the beloved community God created and longs to see live in harmony.

2

A Spirit of Love and
Truth Which Remembers

On January 30, 1956, a month and a half after the beginning of the bus boycott in Montgomery, Alabama, the home of Martin Luther King, Jr. was bombed. Dr. King was speaking at a church meeting, when he heard the news. He sped home to find his wife Coretta and their two month old daughter Yolanda unharmed. The bomb had exploded on the porch and left broken glass all over the living room.

The tension had been in the air since Rosa Parks refused to give up her bus seat to a white man and was arrested. Dr. King had received many threats. When that bomb went off, many people were ready to fight back. A crowd gathered outside King's house. One man challenged a policeman: "You got your thirty-eight, and I got mine. Let's shoot it out." Young men armed themselves with broken bottles and verbally abused the police.

Dr. King came out of his house and stood on the broken porch. His house was almost destroyed and his family could have been killed. He looked at the crowd and said: "My wife and baby are all right. I want you to go home and put down your weapons. We cannot solve this problem through retaliatory violence. . . . We must love our white brothers, no matter what they do to us. We must make them know that we love them. Jesus still cries out across the centuries, 'Love your enemies.' This is what we must live by. We must meet hate with love."

Slowly, people began to leave. Later on, a policeman told a reporter, "I'll be honest with you. I was terrified. I owe my life to that nigger preacher, and so do all the other white people who were there."[3]

Dr. King chose to remember who his persecutors were and to act according to that reality. Instead of giving in to the temptation to respond with further violence, he chose to respond with love and respect and to continue the struggle for justice in that way.

Nonviolence is an attitude and a spirit of genuine love and truth toward all people in every situation which helps us to remember who we are and who we are called to be. Nonviolence is the peace and calm of heart in which we love ourselves, our neighbors and God. It is the act of choosing life. It means living out of a disarmed heart. It is a way of acting which resists and refuses to cooperate with evil and injustice and responds to each act of violence with good will and love and a willingness to suffer oneself rather than inflict suffering on others.

There are four points worth noting which together comprise this spirit and way of life: (1) remembering and acting out of our basic identities, (2) unconditional love which accepts suffering in order to right wrongs and serves others humbly, (3) active resistance to violence and injustice through courageous truth-seeking, and (4) prayer.

The first and last step along the way of nonviolence begins with remembering that we are all God's children, all of us equal brothers and sisters, and that we are meant to love one another. From this worldview and understanding, all our acts follow. This remembering is itself the daily act of recalling our basic identities and living out of them. This remembering means constantly returning to and accepting the peace of heart that God offers to each of us. The peace of heart that God gives to us, if we continually choose to accept it and be faithful to it, disarms us. We accept God's disarming love and remember who we are when we meditate on the reality of God, choose life, and love ourselves as we are, beloved sons and daughters of God.

The choice for life is every decision not to use coercive, harmful force and not to threaten to use violence, no matter what the situation, no matter how much violence faces one. This is the basic choice of nonviolence: to choose life, no matter what the cost for oneself, no matter what the situation. Nonviolence is total noncooperation with violence in the face of violence. It is returning evil with good and insisting that we are all equal, all God's children. Nonviolence is every act of positive goodwill.

The second point in the way of nonviolence is that it is a spirit and force of love, love which is unconditional, nonretaliatory and sacrificial, which stands up and says "No" to violence, and "Yes" to life. Centuries ago, the Greeks used three words for love: *eros* which connoted romantic love and reciprocation, *philia* which expressed intimate affection between friends or the love which is returned because one is loved, and *agape* which meant understanding, redeeming goodwill toward all women and men that seeks nothing in return. *Agape* means disinterested love in which the individual seeks not his or her own good, but the good of his or her neighbors. Nonviolence includes the fullness of *agape,* all positive, active love for true human good in ways that help and cause no harm to others.

Theologian Charles McCarthy defines two main characteristics of *agape:* (1) a willingness to suffer and take the violence of others without the desire for retaliation in order to overcome evil, and (2) a willingness to serve without the desire for reciprocation.[4] These are the steps which we take once we remember that we are loved children of God. We try to right wrongs by loving others as they are, our own brothers and sisters. We do this by accepting suffering rather than inflicting it and by serving others without any hope of service in return. Unconditional, nonretaliatory love seeks to end the suffering of others, to end violence and injustice anywhere. Nonviolence is the willingness, the choice, and the act of taking on the violence of others, suffering through it without retaliating by returning violence for violence and freeing others from the trap of violence so that they can love and be loved in return. In this way of life, one never strikes back, but stands straight, full of love and respect for others. By choosing to suffer through violence, to receive violence without turning back and to return it with love, one can help break the seemingly endless spiral of violence and overcome it, converting it into love.

Agape also includes an active and total life of service toward those who are unable to pay one back, a service which does not demand service in return, a service which is both humble and pure, engrained in one's being as an attitude and a lifestyle. This service is a commitment to those in need and meets those needs, bringing life and justice in the process.

Active nonviolent love which is *agape* is a love for all people, especially those labeled as "enemies," those of us who are blinded into committing and living out of violence and injustice, those of us who are trapped into the world of harming others and ourselves. Martin Luther King, Jr. stressed that "nonviolence does not seek to defeat or humiliate the 'opponent,' but to win friendship and understanding," and "is directed against forces of evil rather than against persons who happen to be doing the evil."[5] King saw the principle of *agape* at the center of nonviolence and defined *agape* as disinterested love especially towards the "enemy-neighbor" from whom no good could be expected in return, only hostility and persecution. King explained it further:

> *Agape* is not a weak, passive love. It is love in action. *Agape* is love seeking to preserve and create community. It is insistence on community even when one seeks to break it. *Agape* is a willingness to sacrifice in the interest of mutuality. *Agape* is a willingness to go to any length to restore community. It is a willingness to forgive, not seven times, but seventy times seven to restore community. If I respond to hate I do nothing but intensify the cleavage in broken community. I can only close the gap in broken community by meeting hate with love. If I meet hate with hate, I become depersonalized, because creation is so designed that my personality can only be fulfilled in the context of community. . . . *Agape* means a recognition of the fact that all life is interrelated. All humanity is involved in a single process, and all men and women are brothers and sisters. To the degree that I harm my brother, no matter what he is doing to me, to that extent I am harming myself. . . . If you harm me, you harm yourself. . . . When I am commanded to love, I am commanded to restore community, to resist injustice and to meet the needs of my brothers and sisters.[6]

Capturing the heart of *agape,* King knew that nonviolence "avoids not only external physical violence, but also internal violence of spirit." It is grounded in a peaceful, disarmed heart. It is an attitude and a spirit free from violence, which frees one to love and to be loved, to be oneself, to be a beloved child of God.

The spirit and way of nonviolence also includes a third point, active resistance to violence and injustice through courageous truth-seeking. As the union of love and truth, nonviolence is a spirit and a way of active resistance to violence and injustice, to all that works against love and truth. Nonviolence is not passivism or apathy; it is action that disarms, reconciles, and helps others to see the reality that all are equal and meant to be treated with love and respect. It is always active, seeking to change evil into good by the creative and courageous love and truth which it is rooted and grounded in. To be nonviolent means to insist on love and truth everywhere and thus to spend one's life loving others and overcoming evil with good.

Nonviolence as active resistance to violence and injustice moves on the personal, family, communal and national level, creating conversion, reconciliation and community at every stage. On the personal and family levels, nonviolence can mean acting in a spirit and an attitude of love and truth that consciously confronts violence and selfishness in today's world by drawing it out of others, by inspiring others to change their hearts, attitudes and lifestyles. It will be action that provokes a response in order to draw out latent violence in structures and in hearts and it will free others from the bondage of violence.

Organized communal nonviolence can reveal the power of love and truth on a massive scale. There are many forms of active nonviolence which endeavor to dissolve violence in others' hearts and in one's own heart, and to change accepted patterns and practices of society which are unjust and inherently violent. Such organized movements which can be instruments of the spirit of nonviolence include protests, the non-cooperation of strikes, boycotts, and tax resistance, and the creative civil disobedience of sit-ins. National nonviolent campaigns, such as the nonviolent resistance in Denmark during World War II, the nonviolent struggle for independence led by Gandhi in India, and the civil rights movement in the United States during the 1960's, have demonstrated the great potential of large scale nonviolent love. The personal and communal witness of nonviolence, while beginning with a spirit of love and truth in one's own heart, is always other-centered and public. In the end, nonviolence is an extroversion that increases love and truth in the whole human family.

Nonviolence as public, active resistance to injustice and violence seeks to bring about the genuine good of all concerned, as Martin Luther King, Jr. explained: "The nonviolent resister must often express his protest through noncooperation or boycotts, but he realizes that these are not ends themselves; they are merely means to awaken a sense of moral shame in the opponent. The end is redemption and reconciliation. The aftermath of nonviolence is the creation of the beloved community, while the aftermath of violence is tragic bitterness."[7] In nonviolent resistance, conversion occurs when the aggressor sees the common humanity in the nonviolent resisters who are courageously suffering while resisting violence and demanding change.

But nonviolence always begins in the stillness of each person's heart, as he or she seeks peace and tries to live in a spirit of love. As a spirit and an attitude of love for all others, nonviolence is, at the same time, a spirit and an attitude which courageously lives in and seeks truth, that which is right and just. This courageous truth-seeking is a spirit and a way of radical honesty with oneself and others, a way that does not permit lying or cooperating with untruth. As opposed to the moments of violence when we deny the truth and choose death, nonviolence seeks to accept and fully embrace the truth and is thus always life-giving. In nonviolence as resistance, the force of love allows others to see what is true without resorting to methods of coercion, and enables others and those trying to be nonviolent to step more fully into the world of truth. In the personal way of nonviolence, courageous truthseeking can only be founded in a radical humility freed from self-righteousness and in a spirit of openness.

Nonviolence is a way of living in truth and talking truth to others. Truth is often lost because our pride gives way to lies, hatred, and the harm, both physical and spiritual, which people do to one another. Gandhi taught that Truth is God. Truth is to be reverenced, to be loved in humility, and to become the ground and the rock of existence. In our efforts to seek truth, we patiently listen to others and accept any new truth with a spirit of peace. We will immediately change our ways when necessary and we will eagerly suffer when necessary in order to help ourselves and others to see the truth more clearly.

The fourth point to note is that nonviolence, a way of life, is a life of prayer, a way of living with greater openness to God, centered on God, loving God, living out a spirit of great faith and hope. The road of nonviolence is a road of prayer to our ever-present God. It is a peaceful way of daily, regular meditation which fills us with great peace and life in a world of strife and turmoil, and inspires and disposes us to a greater willingness to love others, to suffer joyfully in order to right wrongs, to serve others humbly, and to remain faithful. It means embracing the loneliness of life by entering into daily solitude and there finding God. From this life of prayer and solitude of heart, we are able to be with one another, to develop our relationships, and to find peace with one another.

Every act of nonviolent love helps us to remember again that we are all children of God, brothers and sisters of one another. With a sincere heart and a faithful desire to do the will of God, we can place all our trust in God and God will lead us as we try to become nonviolent because God is nonviolent and has promised us these things. When we act nonviolently, when we act in love and in truth, God is present.

This simple nonviolence can infuse one's mind, soul, heart and body and provide a method of life. Anyone can begin to cultivate a nonviolent spirit and life and begin to live in the world of nonviolence. This way of life is not a strategy or a technique with definite steps and choices involved, or an ideology, but a peaceful spirit and a path to be followed. Although human beings can never become perfectly nonviolent in this life, through great discipline, prayer and sacrifice they can asymptotically approach nonviolence of heart and mind with each small act of love and humble service to the truth. With every risk of love and truth we take, no matter how small, we free others and ourselves further into a more meaningful world.

When we remember who we are and act out of that reality, then our little acts of love and truth which make up our way of nonviolence will reconcile us to one another and transform our entire way of living with one another. We will begin to find harmony in ourselves and in our relationships with others as well as in our world.

Martin Luther King, Jr. responded freely and spontaneously in the manner of nonviolence on January 30, 1956 when his house was bombed, and on many other occasions afterward, because he made a fundamental, radical choice to follow the way of nonviolence, no matter how difficult that appeared and no matter how apparently futile. It was a choice he was continuously asked to make throughout his life. Because we are weak and so often forget who we are and what we are about, some of us may feel moved to profess publicly a commitment to the way of nonviolence in order to help focus our hearts and to begin or to renew our daily choice to follow the way of nonviolence. Before looking at what is involved in such a fundamental choice, a vow of nonviolence, the meaning of vows needs to be explored.

3

A Channel of Grace

Vows have long been a part of the Judaeo-Christian tradition, from baptismal vows to the vows of marriage or of the religious life to private, devotional vows taken in line with a person's calling. A vow is a deliberate, religiously binding, solemn promise made to God concerning some good taken after serious preparation and in full freedom.[8] It is a pledge to be faithful to a way of life, a dedication to a way of life even through trials, difficulties and temptations. A vow can act as a channel of God's grace in one's life.

Vows are a sign of commitment to a new way of life, the beginning of a whole new journey that will be the remainder of one's life. They are channels, instruments, of God's grace already working in the person. As channels of grace, they act as open doors which allow the loving action of God to flow in and through a person.

A vow as a channel of grace can be a great support to the person, helping the person come into the way of life he or she has chosen and allowing that new way to be engrained in the person's spirit and attitude so that even when difficulties arise, one's natural response will be in the manner of the vow, free and spontaneous. A vow is guaranteed to arouse difficulties and provoke danger because it is the pledge to another way of life, a deeper way that runs against the grain of human society. It is professed in order to help one maintain this life of contrast to the way of the world and contradiction to the normal way of proceeding, to the acceptable values of society.

The tradition of the vow appears in Hebrew Scripture, when the vow was accompanied by a sacrifice, often the burnt offering of a ram. In affliction, when the people of Israel needed the special help of God, their vows, which were temporary, included not only a sacrificial offering but acts of self-denial. Fasting was a frequent accompaniment of a vow. Psalms of thanksgiving sing Yahweh's praise when the vow was fulfilled and deliverance from the affliction effected. The psalmist sings in the 65th Psalm, "I will go into thy house with burnt offerings. I will pay thee my vows which my lips have uttered." The Psalm ends with praise for the deliverance, "Blessed be God who has not turned away my prayer nor his mercy for me."

Christians have always been making promises through their baptism and their baptismal renewal since before the writing of the New Testament. Baptism is itself the promise, the vow, to follow Jesus and his way of life and to reject Satan and his way of life. Vows arose in the history of the Christian community as instruments to refresh and renew the ideals and the call of discipleship and commitment which had become lukewarm. Historically, in Christian tradition, vows have been instruments of recall and repentance, encouraged by the Christian community in order to return Christians to the hard road, the high ideals and daily realities, crosses and hardships of the Gospel message. The vows were intended to and succeeded in shaking some Christians out of their comfortable lifestyles and into the uncomfortable lifestyle of companionship with Jesus. Over the centuries, after vows sparked the fire of renewal among those who professed them and may have helped maintain the faithfulness of the community, they appeared to lose some of their spark as many communities began to become more stable and secure and less dependent on God. Many who professed vows to the strict discipleship to which God calls us fell into the temptations and trappings of mediocre, less evangelical lifestyles. Many of the vowed in history were less poor, less chaste and less obedient (for example) to the demands of the Gospel than the unvowed.

For Christians, a vow is a pledge of commitment to the promises made for oneself at baptism. It is a pledge to begin a more faithful life of imitation and discipleship to Jesus Christ, a pledge to witness to the way of life which Jesus lived and revealed as the most fully human. Every Christian is really called to the vowed life, to the way of life introduced by Jesus. The basic vow for the Christian is a vow of allegiance to the kingdom of God as revealed in Jesus Christ. Vows of truth, nonviolence, poverty, chastity and obedience are part and parcel of the Christian commitment or vow of allegiance made at baptism. A vow is an explicit reminder of who I am called to be and thus an ever present admission of dependence on God if we are to be who we want to be.

Vows are a celebration of a state that *already* exists; a celebration of the way one already lives; a celebration of the commitment one has grasped to be one's very self, to live as the child God has called that person to be; a celebration of a fact—the fact that one is a Christian which means a nonviolent follower of the nonviolent Lord. Vows are public witnesses to the Reality present in one's heart. They are public expressions of the unity that exists, of the conversion that has occurred. Specific vows do not or should not create a level of higher commitment to following Jesus. Every Christian is called to live the life of the vows, such as nonviolence, poverty, chastity and obedience to God. These demands are demands in the life of everyone who pledges allegiance to Christ and his way of life. Those who publicly vow themselves are witnessing to the reality which already exists in their hearts, and are thus professing their faith and gratitude to God and inviting others to join them in this way of life.

A vow for the Christian or any truth-seeker is thus a reminder not of his or her Pelagian duty to perform, but of God's infinite love for him or her and for every single human being. Acts of Love and Truth will naturally flow from this reminder, this vow, and be fruit that grows from the Reality which the vow represents, the gift given by God. One will take a vow to some Godlike way of life, such as nonviolence, to remind oneself of God's gift of nonviolent love. Vows will help us remember who we are, what God has done for us, and who we are called to be. The vows can not be lived separate from the faith commitment which is one's very heart and soul, which keeps one searching for the Holy One.

In reality, the Christian does not "make" a vow; he or she affirms the reality of a vow already made by God. God has vowed to love and support us. Therefore, by pledging ourselves to poverty, chastity, obedience or nonviolence as God's way of life, we are not "creating" the vowed situation or relationship: we are merely witnessing to the fact of its reality in our lives. The vow should not be looked upon as something we *do* for God, but as something God *is doing* in our lives. Concerning the vow of nonviolence, Christians have already experienced the disarming love of Jesus, a love which is nonviolent, pure, preferential for the poor and radically obedient to God. To profess a vow is an act of witnessing to God's love for us. We profess vows to God's way of life—in this case, God's nonviolence—in order to be a sign of that Love in the world. Vows help us to witness to all that God is doing for us and for the whole human family.

Any vow is a formal dedication of oneself to a way of life in imitation of God and is pledged to God, but also to all humanity, one's community and oneself. Vows by their very nature should free a person to become more fully human, alive and at the service of others. Vows are thus other-directed and yet serve to maintain a person's freedom in the way of life chosen—forever. They become instruments of freedom and release the person to be the person God calls and wants him or her to be.

While a vow can help a person to hold fast to the great commitment of life, to an expression of truth and love, as a channel of freedom and release, it is not therefore some kind of legalism. A vow does not begin a life of rigid adherence to a set of laws, but rather breaks any rigid set of laws in one's life and stimulates a person to risk development in one particular facet of life, to risk growth in God's spiritual way of life. Without being legalistic, they bind a person rather to a higher law, God's strict law of love and truth which demands unshakable insecurity, freedom and dependence on God. Because of its spiritual and practical nature, a vow will be dangerous and risky, and ultimately impossible to fulfill in one's life. It becomes the ideal by which one continually acts each and every day in thought, word, and deed, a goal perpetually pursued and practiced at one and the same time which is still not a rigid application of a law. Although there is always some more fundamental level—God's higher law of love and truth—to which a person tries to cling in the vowed life, a vow is a promise to risk and experiment with great freedom in one's life in an area that is hard, demanding and usually impossible to achieve. It is never easy to attempt to live out a vow, yet the vow itself can give one the energy and encouragement to persevere in freedom. Vows do not create stability and security in one's life, but the radical instability and insecurity of strict dependence on God. This is the freedom which vows can release for a person, a radical dependence on God, a strict obedience to God and not to the ways of the world. To be fully human, we can no longer rely on human structures or institutions but on God alone. Vows as instruments of God's grace should release us and free us from human structures and institutions into that world of complete dependence on God, into the world of emptiness so that God will live in us. Vows thus release us from all human laws, all human ways of operating, and set us free into God's way of life, which God has intended for all humans.

Vows are therefore never coercive by nature and do not subject a person to some *punishing* authority—whether the Church, a religious community, or the vowed person's own consciousness—which can enforce the vow and punish infractions. Fear and coercion are antithetical to the vowed life; they have no place in the nature of a vow. A vow is freely professed and lived, not made in fear or lived in fear, not made under coercion or lived under coercion. If a vow is made under fear or coercion, it is not true to the nature of the vow. Fear and coercion have no place in the discernment of whether or not to profess a vow or in the living of a vow. When one suspects fear or coercion in the vowed life, one is to act against this in the freedom of grace which the vow encourages, and to live the life God desires. God does not act through fear or coercion. Vows, as channels of grace, cannot be lived within fear or coercion either.

Like baptismal promises, vows express the kind of person we want to be. Unlike an oath which usually invokes God as a witness to truth (and thus implies that God may coercively punish the person), baptismal promises and evangelical vows are made to God and one another as expressions of the deepest desires about the kind of persons we want to be. They are therefore prayers of petition, asking God's help to become what we believe God has called us to be.

When done in community, vows can become a bond of love, as marriage vows bind two people in love to love. The vows become part of the friendship that is community and become invitations to call one another to faithfulness, to be the persons God intended us to be. A vow pledged in community may make the commitment more memorable, that is, engrained more deeply into one's being as an attitude to live out of in a fresh, free, life-giving manner. Communal celebration of a vow to a way of life can be part of the vow itself, providing spiritual motivation, support, strength, and freedom to the person taking it, so that the person will be able to throw himself or herself into the most challenging situations which have the potential to break the vow and inspire conversion. Such a sacramentalization of a vow acted in community can enforce one's promise all the more and provide needed strength for the most challenging situations. A communal celebration of a vow can also provide a great witness and source of strength to the community itself that is gathered, and thus provide a channel of God's grace to every person who takes part in the event, to every person who becomes a witness of what God is doing in the newly vowed person.

A vow professed in community and lived out with God, one's community and ultimately the entire human family, can become a great sign in itself to the world by calling the world to a new way of life, a better way of life, freedom and the inner peace of being the people God has called us to be. For this reason alone, a vow has the possibility of being a great tool for the service, disarmament and redemption of humanity and is thus worth serious consideration and discernment by all.

A vow publicly symbolizes the acceptance of and commitment to God's call to be who we are. A vow to God's way of life, made in freedom and having nothing to do with fear and coercion, is fundamentally a gift from God, and faithfulness to such a vow is also a gift from God. It can be maintained only through diligent effort and constant attention, but fundamentally through God's grace. Any vow to a way of life is impossible to keep—by its very nature—without God. Yet through one's desire and will to cling to the pledge, one may be freed to a faithful fulfillment of the path chosen, embraced, or, better, recognized as already existing. There is always this paradox involved in professing a vow: it will help one to live a seemingly impossible way of life, and yet it is not one's doing at all that sees to the continued fulfillment of the vow but the work (grace) of God. The vow proclaims what God has done for a person and reminds the person continually of what God has done and is doing. The vow is a reminder to the person that God is the one who is acting, that God is living and moving within that person.

Vows are channels of grace which help us to remember.

For the apparently impossible task of living a life of nonviolence, of being the nonviolent person God has intended that person to be, a vow may prove to be a great help. In our age of nuclear weapons, hunger and violence, some may desire to symbolize their life commitment to active nonviolence by professing a vow.

4

Great Love in a Time of Great Need

Nonviolence maintains that violent force is not morally or religiously acceptable or justifiable on any grounds. Every human being suffers from and is a victim of violence, needs to be freed from violence, and can become more nonviolent. To be fully human in today's world is to be nonviolent, to be loving, reconciling, and healing for others. There are many reasons why one might be moved to consider vowing nonviolence. In order to discuss the reasons why some may be called to vowed nonviolence, it may be helpful to examine why one might be moved by the forces of evil which are at work in our day and age. A meditation on the violence of the world may help to remind us that the violence we speak of is not some academic matter for discussion; it is real. It is not some abstraction, not something that does not concern us. Violence committed anywhere toward anyone is violence done to us, to our brothers and sisters. It hurts both victims and victimizers, and needs to be overcome by our love, by our willingness to take on suffering. The violence which we commit through our governments is real and we must accept the blame for it and put an end to it. After briefly looking at the realities of violence in our age, we shall consider some specific personal and communal advantages and graces a vow of nonviolence has to offer. A vow of nonviolence is a great grace being offered by God to many people in these days as a means of reform and renewal on all levels: spiritual, physical, personal, intellectual, theological, interpersonal, communal and international. As we explore reasons why some might choose to vow nonviolence, we will see that, in the end, people have begun to see that God, as revealed in Jesus, is nonviolent and they want to be more like God, to do as God does.

The personal and international crises of today's world call for a completely new way of living, for some, a vowed life of complete disposal to the will of God in the way and the work of active, nonviolent love. In 1906, when Mohandas Gandhi spoke to a crowd of South Africans about their struggle for justice, he called for a personal commitment, a total response to the nonviolent work of justice and said that if ever a crisis in community affairs warranted a vow, now was the time. In a time and world where over fifty thousand people die of dramatic starvation every day, where over twenty million human beings have been killed through legal abortion in the United States alone since January 22, 1973, where wars rage on with no end in sight, where torture is practiced in many countries as a national policy, where military spending appears to know no limit and oppresses the poor into destitution and death, where nations execute their prisoners and give out tickets to watch the electrocutions (such as in California), it is necessary for some to make the commitment of vowed nonviolence in order to be a hopeful sign of God's love for every human being. This is the value of the vow: to witness, to be a sign of another reality in a world of violence. The vow does not create a new reality; it just makes explicit what is implicitly Christian, that God loves every human being unconditionally and invites us to love the same way.

The human family appears to be trapped into the endless spiral of violence, of injustice, hatred, lies and fear. The radical evil, the great sin of apathy in the face of relievable human suffering and misery, continues its effort to take control over human society.[9] The spirit and work of violence cause people to forget who we are and divide us up. At the present moment in world history, millions of human beings around the world are engaged in the preparation, the study and planning, the strategizing and manuevering of war, as well as in the actual fighting of war. Governments, cultures, and military forces have become abstracted from the actual killings. Military forces are honored and exalted as serving their country and the world through the act of preparing the fighting, the annihilation and the slaughter of other human beings. The ultimate purpose in any military force is always the killing of other human beings. With the existence and continued building of nuclear weapons, the possibility of killing millions of individual human beings in a nuclear war has now become a fact. The time, money, and human talent spent on building and maintaining these weapons actually oppress millions of human beings in third world countries into poverty, hunger and early deaths. Nuclear weapons, the preparation to use violence, and the use of violence always leads to death, mourning families, despair, destruction, broken families, wounded people who will suffer for the rest of their lives, orphans, widows and widowers, and casualties on all levels of society. War, the nuclear arms race, and violence result from blind obedience, naive acceptance, tacit indifference, or complete unrealization and misunderstanding of the taking of human lives, the actual killing of other peoples. They also are the result of an unwillingness to forgive and to be healed from the violence used against each person who participates in a war at some point in his or her life. War, the nuclear arms race, and all violence are inhuman, immoral and wrong.

In the twentieth century, organized and systemic violence has reached global perspectives. In World Wars I and
II, millions of men, women, and children all over the world
died in senseless horror. In World War I, religions and
church groups gave support to their governments for mass
murder. In World War II, fifty million human beings were
killed. In America and Europe, this war was declared "just"
by clergy on both sides.[10] In German concentration camps,
millions of people were incinerated and killed. Fire storms
from allied air power killed 155,000 men, women, and children in Dresden in February 1943, 50,000 in Hamburg in
August 1943, 12,000 in Darmstadt in September 1944, and
25,000 in Berlin in February 1945. On March 9, 1945, 333
B-29s destroyed sixteen square miles of Tokyo with incen-
diary bombs and killed 130,000 men, women and children.
The next night, 313 planes, using napalm, set fire to
Nagoya, Japan's third largest city. On May 23 and 25, B-
29s were used to begin another fire storm which killed thousands and destroyed seventeen additional square miles of
Tokyo. As the fire bombings continued in Japan, killing
thousands more, *Time* magazine described the fire bombings as a "dream come true."[11]

On Monday, August 6, 1945, the atomic bomb was
dropped on Hiroshima, killing over 100,000 men, women,
and children. Hiroshima, the seventh largest city in Japan,
had been spared the summer's fire bombings so that the
U.S. military planners could see the effects of the atomic
bomb on a relatively large and untouched city.[12] The bomb
dropped by the United States on the city of Nagasaki three
days later killed over 30,000 more men, women and
children.

In the arms race that has developed since 1945, the
United States and the Soviet Union have learned to pro-
duce hydrogen bombs, which have the destructive force of

over fifty times the bomb used on Hiroshima, and an enormous stockpile of other nuclear weapons.[13] Great Britain, France, China and India have also tested nuclear weapons. Argentina, Canada, West Germany, Israel, Italy, Japan, Pakistan, South Africa, Sweden and Switzerland can all build nuclear weapons. Other countries could develop nuclear weapons within five or ten years, including Australia, Austria, Belgium, Brazil, Denmark, Egypt, Finland, Iraq, Libya, Netherlands, Norway, South Korea, Spain, Taiwan and Yugoslavia. According to one estimate, the number of existing nuclear warheads is over 50,000, enough to destroy every city in the world several times over.[14] The United States can destroy every city of 100,000 or more people in the Soviet Union at least thirty-six times. The Soviet Union can destroy every U.S. city at least eleven times.[15] In the continuous effort to build more bombs, over $500 billion is spent annually on world armaments. If one-tenth were diverted to the underdeveloped world, it would be more than the total amount estimated by the World Bank that would be needed to wipe out world hunger. Well over 100 million dollars is spent every day on armaments worldwide. Since World War II, the direct cost of the arms race has well exceeded 6,000 billion dollars ($6,000,000,000,000). The total megatonage now deployed is estimated to be equivalent to over one million Hiroshima bombs—or three tons of conventional explosives for every man, woman and child on earth. About twenty-five percent of the world's scientific personnel are engaged in military-related pursuits.[16]

As the money, time, and energy spent on building weapons to kill people all over the world increases, men, women, and children are further deprived of basic living needs, such as food, clothing, shelter, medicine, or education. Millions of men, women and children live in absolute poverty and are starving to death, homeless, naked, jobless, sick, imprisoned, orphaned, alienated or lost. By the year 2000, over 470 million people will be living in this kind of absolute total poverty.[17] The nuclear arms race and the works of violence subject and oppress the majority of the human family into early and unjust deaths.

Nationalistic, conventional warfare continues to kill and do violence to peoples everywhere. The war over the Falkland Islands between the Argentine and British governments in 1982; the U.S. invasion of Grenada; the wars in Ireland, Afghanistan, Cambodia, Africa, the Philippines, India, Vietnam, Korea, Iran and Iraq and Central America: all have brought misery, oppression and death to countless people. The death squads of El Salvador alone have murdered well over 50,000 men, women, and children since 1979. The victims of these wars always tend to be poor, oppressed peoples. For example, on May 14, 1980, six hundred people, mostly women and children, were massacred by Salvadoran and Honduran troops in the waters of the Sumpul River. When I lived in El Salvador, during the summer of 1985, I often stood with poor Salvadorans who had lost their homes and family members and friends because of the war, and watched and listened as government airplanes bombed and machine gunned a nearby mountain. The horror of war is a terrible reality that must be overcome. The United States continues to support the violence and wars orchestrated by the Salvadoran and Guatemalan governments, and other Latin American nations, as well as violent efforts to overthrow the Nicaraguan government and to kill more poor people.

Abortion, capital punishment, and torture also continue to kill thousands of people. In the United States, 1,600,000 unborn children die every year by legal abortion, well over 4,000 children murdered every day. More babies are killed by abortion annually in the U.S. than the combined populations of Miami, Kansas City and Minneapolis. Every year more and more men and women are killed through gas chambers, lethal injections, electric chairs, and other forms of murder in the United States and in several other countries for their crimes. Torture, the use of violence on individual human beings, is a common practice by many governments around the world. Also, millions of children, women and men suffer the violence of displacement, becoming refugees in their own homelands or in other countries. Sexism and sexist structures oppress women throughout the world. Racism continues to kill, especially in South Africa, and divides the human family.

In Western culture, violence pervades almost every aspect of life. Television programs and movies promote the violent lifestyle and portray violent people as heroic and admirable. Magazines advertise the network of violence and spread violence. Some cartoons, toys, comic books, and other products for children promote and advocate violence.

One problem in our world is the effort among the wealthier classes to maintain their wealth and to make more money as well as the desire to possess money among many people in many areas. The largest owners of the world's wealth and natural resources, the banking and investment systems throughout the world, all seek to maintain, to control and to increase their wealth, often influencing governments to protect their assets by threatening or using violence.

Many people feel helpless or apathetic in the face of such violence. Cultural indifference or promotion of violence encourages people to believe there is nothing that can be done to prevent violence. Indeed, sanity, according to society's definition, has come to mean cultural approval and conformity, no matter how serious the complicity in violence.[18]

The terrible evil of violence must be faced, again and again, confronted and recognized as damaging. When violence appears to prevail as the dominant attitude and the natural inclination, people must begin to act against it, to remember who we are and what we are about, and to become nonviolent in every situation. We must remember to and continue to love one another. Instead of striving for success, fame, wealth, pleasure and power, we must seek to live according to the purpose for which we were created: to know, love, and serve God and one another, in this life and in the next. A movement for peace and justice is sweeping through the churches and religious groups around the world. People are beginning to stand up for justice and mercy by way of active nonviolence. The Sojourners community and the Catholic Worker movement in the United States, Pax Christi, the International Catholic movement for peace, the Community of the Ark in France and "Servicio Paz y Justicia" in Latin America are just a few of the signs of hope and light shining around the world at this very moment.

In order to begin or to renew the steadfast commitment to active love and peaceful resistance, some may choose to profess a vow of nonviolence. In order to help others to remember the foundation on which they were created, to channel their energy to God, to do what God wants, to love and serve the truth wholeheartedly and steadfastly, to serve suffering humanity, to deny oneself and to accept suffering rather than inflict it in the process, and to follow God in God's disarming, compassionate way, some may make the radical choice of nonviolence as a way of life. In order to continue to resist this culture of death and violence and its hatred and fear of life, some may take this step to express a fundamental choice for life.

Besides the great need for great love in our time, there are many other personal, practical reasons why a person may consider professing a vow of nonviolence. A vow of nonviolence may prove to be psychologically helpful and supportive in a world which does not actively promote nonviolence. A vow of nonviolence can provide an individual with an anchor to hold fast to a way of God. A vow of nonviolence can encapsulate the commitment to perpetual nonviolence in one's being, behavior, attitude and actions, in all one's thoughts, words and deeds. Vowed nonviolence may become a grace and a new channel for the Spirit of God to work through his people in today's world to bring about greater reconciliation between people and God.

When one is tempted to use violence, a vow of nonviolence may become the instrument which holds a person to the way of love. For example, a person vowed to nonviolence may be confronted with unexpected challenges when visiting or working in a third world region where the daily struggle for survival amid terrible poverty and oppression has often turned to guns and guerrilla warfare. A group of demonstrators opposing the work of a nuclear weapons facility might be tempted to respond violently and to threaten physical injury to workers and guards. In a personal attack of mugging, arrest or a threat, one may begin to respond with violence or to be passive. In any of these cases, one's response may more likely be nonviolent, active yet firm and loving, if one has the reminder of a vow of nonviolence.

In the face of violence, in the moment of temptation when violence seems like the best response, one can return to one's vow of nonviolence, and rethink such a decision, saying: "When I was at prayer or on retreat listening to God's voice and following God through the choice of life-long nonviolence, I vowed myself to accept and live out God's way of peace and active love. So now in this confrontation, I will not regress or go back on my decision to be nonviolent. I will resist violence through love, forgiveness, and my own willingness to take on suffering rather than inflicting it." A vow of nonviolence may be the instrument of God which can encourage faithfulness in difficult situations by inspiring faith in God who may appear absent in the face of such a threat. A person vowed to nonviolence will be unable to take part in or support any violence, on any level, in any form. The vowed person of nonviolence will avoid harming or threatening to harm any other person, and will instead strive to be honest, to love others, and to maintain a humble, prayerful heart centered on God and God's kingdom. In response to violence, a vow will encourage the person of nonviolence to remain steadfast saying: "I will have nothing to do with violence in any way, shape or form. I will not partake in the threat of violence or oppression. I will oppose it actively and dramatically with all my being by following the principles of nonviolence. I will cultivate a spirit of love and truth in my heart and be faithful to the commands of my God."

The people who joined Francis of Assisi in his Third Order pledged never to carry or use weapons, or to take the oath of fealty—steps which led eventually, according to historians, to the downfall of feudalism and fratricidal wars. Gandhi led his co-workers in a vow of nonviolence which helped his liberation campaigns to change the history of the world. In our own time, Martin Luther King, Jr. understood the need and the importance of a serious commitment to nonviolence. In his campaign for civil rights in Birmingham, Alabama in 1963, each participant was required to sign a Commitment Card which made the following promise:

> I hereby pledge myself—my person and my body—to the nonviolent movement. Therefore I will keep the following ten commandments:
>
>   1. Meditate daily on the teachings and life of Jesus.
>   2. Remember always that the nonviolent movement in Birmingham seeks justice and reconciliation—not victory.
>   3. Walk and talk in the manner of love, for God is love.
>   4. Pray daily to be used by God in order that all men and women might be free.
>   5. Sacrifice personal wishes in order that all men and women might be free.
>   6. Observe with both friend and foe the ordinary rules of courtesy.
>   7. Seek to perform regular service for others and for the world.
>   8. Refrain from the violence of fist, tongue, or heart.
>   9. Strive to be in good spiritual and bodily health.
>   10. Follow the directions of the movement and of the captain on a demonstration.
>
> I sign this pledge, having seriously considered what I do and with the determination and will to persevere.[19]

Martin Luther King, Jr. spent his life pleading the case for nonviolence as the way of social change and conversion from hate to disinterested love for all people. The efforts of nonviolent action were not to be effective, he felt, if there was any spirit of hate in the demonstrator. He was convinced that hatred and anger toward others were useless acts of violence, but he did allow for hatred and anger toward the actual injustices and the violence. He sought to make friends, to reconcile and to build new relationships between black and white people of peace based in God and Christian love. He understood the importance of a serious commitment in active nonviolence. In the nuclear age when nonviolent resistance is so necessary, a vow of nonviolence may be just as important to maintain a steadfast, persevering spirit of energetic nonviolence.

A vow of nonviolence can also mark a clean start in a person's life, a way for a person to begin life again. It can be an instrument that gives one the courage and the strength to act and to speak nonviolently. It can be an instrument of renewal for someone who wants to begin a deeper life of nonviolence. It can help affirm one's mission and one's way of life. It can consecrate a person's life of experimenting and practicing nonviolence, and provide a spiritual framework from which one can live. It can also provide a check against conformity or silent acceptance of the status quo if someone finds that he or she is not living up to the commitment of love that he or she desires. It may sting one's conscience and call one to be more loving, humble and truthful. Instead of worrying about the effectiveness of one's life and actions, a vow of nonviolence can be the instrument of perseverance, of letting go of one's personal plans and schemes for effective change by providing a check on this temptation and urging a greater trust in Divine Providence and faithfulness to the will of God.

A vow of nonviolence can be an instrument of liberation and freedom for one to begin living the way one has always wanted to live by formally acknowledging one's acceptance of the way of nonviolence. It may free a person to be unafraid in the face of danger, tension, threats of violence or death, and allow a person to break through the barriers of violence and to take on suffering in order to right wrongs.

Vowing nonviolence can be a new channel of grace for one's community. The public profession of a vow may help spark conversion and renewal in others, help change communal institutions and structures and provide an increase of love among one's community. A public profession of perpetual nonviolence may inspire a stronger commitment to God in others. It may stimulate dialogue and be a sign of hope to people, a witness of another way of life. Vowed nonviolence by many individuals may give birth to many communities of creative, active nonviolence all over the world.

The vow of nonviolence is a great gift from God, an alternative way of living in an age of violence, a channel of renewal, reform, and refreshment, a life-giving means of finding meaning and purpose in an age where meaning in life is easily lost and despair appears pervasive. As an evangelical vow, it can be an expression of and a commitment to being a certain kind of person, leading a certain kind of life. A vow of nonviolence may also function to specify the human *telos,* the end to which we are created, the path we are to follow. This vow, along with vows of poverty, chastity, obedience in community, and truth, may help to clarify and commit us to attributes of what we consider to be a faithful, more human life.

One's great *love* of suffering humanity and for all victims of violence may be another reason for professing wholeheartedly nonviolence. Vowed perpetual nonviolence will be pledged because one loves the entire human family so much, longs never to harm anyone, and desires only to spend one's life serving those who are suffering, taking on suffering in an effort to change society and help others remember who they are. A final reason for professing a vow of nonviolence is not just because of a person's great love for suffering humanity—a love which is really quite imperfect—*but because God loves suffering humanity,* the whole human family, *unconditionally.* The person who receives and accepts this tremendous love of God can witness to it by publicly announcing adherence to this love and Reality.

John Howard Yoder, writing about nonviolence as the way of life for the Christian, states: "The reason for the Christian's being called to live above this world's battles is not that one of the Ten Commandments enjoins us not to kill, or not that Jesus as a new lawgiver orders us to love our enemies. The Christian has been disarmed by God. There is no need for orders to love one's neighbors, beginning in the smallest circle of daily relationships, or one's enemies; the Christian is driven to this by the love of Christ within his or her life."[20] The vow of nonviolence is not an "order" or a "law" which one puts on oneself; instead, it is *a way of witnessing to others how God has disarmed oneself.* By professing a vow of nonviolence, the commitment to continue living out God's nonviolence, a person proclaims to all the world a Reality which already exists, the disarmament of one's being by God and the desire to grow in that loving disarmament.

The vow of nonviolence is *a recognition of who we are*—disarmed people, nonviolent people who have been and are continually being disarmed by God. God has disarmed us and revealed God's way of life—loving, humble nonviolence. By vowing nonviolence, we may be able to help others see how God is disarming them as God continues to disarm us. God is making our hearts nonviolent, forming us into the image of Christ. The vow accepts this work of God and witnesses to God's Spirit of nonviolence as a new way of life. A vow of nonviolence can then indeed be a witness to the *good news* of the nonviolent way in a world where violence appears to reign. A vow of nonviolence may help a person to act with greater love in time of great need and thus further the disarmament of hearts and nations.

5

The Vow of Nonviolence:
A Pledge of Peaceful Resistance
and Active Love

The vow of nonviolence is a channel for God's grace of nonviolence, an instrument of the nonviolent revolution happening in one's heart and being lived out in the grace and freedom of one's life. The vow of nonviolence is for the Christian, most importantly, an expression of one's baptismal vow; it is the public witness to one's baptism as a Christian. It is the acknowledgment and the acceptance of God's grace of nonviolence in one's life, the acceptance of the gift God has given. Besides this, it is the pledge to live the new life committed to the demands of God's gift. Thus, the vow of nonviolence becomes the formal acceptance of what God has done in one's life and a help toward living out that gift and sharing it with others by spreading God's revolution of nonviolence through resistance and contemplation which is love and truth. It is a channel of grace which will aid people in their commitment to a life of love.

To get to the heart of what is happening in the vow of nonviolence, we can begin by looking at the baptismal promises made by Christians and their renewal. Baptismal promises which renounce sin and Satan and profess faith in God and the good news of Jesus Christ admit a person into a new covenant with God. God's gift of faith is fully accepted and embraced and one takes a stand to live this out in gratitude, to witness to what God has done through the gift of faith. The annual renewal of baptismal promises is a series of questions and affirmations which reveal what God has done in faith and how the Christian will continue to accept God's loving action. At the Easter renewal, the presider begins with the invitation: "Now that we have completed our Lenten observance, let us renew the promises we made in baptism when we rejected Satan and his works and promised to serve God faithfully in his holy Catholic Church. Do you reject sin so as to live in the freedom of God's children?" Each person then responds, "I do." "Do you reject the glamor of evil and refuse to be mastered by sin?" "I do." "Do you reject Satan, father of sin and prince of darkness?" "I do." "Do you believe in God, the Father Almighty and Creator of heaven and earth?" "I do." "Do you believe in Jesus Christ, our Lord . . . ?" "I do." "Do you believe in the Holy Spirit . . . the forgiveness of sins, the resurrection of the body and life everlasting?" "I do." "God, the All-Powerful Father of our Lord Jesus Christ, has given us a new birth by water and the Holy Spirit and forgiven all our sins. May he also keep us faithful to our Lord Jesus Christ for ever and ever." "Amen."

The Catholic liturgy of initiation includes rites for renouncing non-Christian worship. In one formula, the celebrant makes a profession of faith and asks an important question: "Christ Jesus alone has the power to protect men and women. Are you determined never to abandon him and return to use N. (Here he names objects which are used superstitiously or other ways of defense which deny the Lordship of Christ.) Nuclear weapons and violence could easily be substituted as ways antithetical to Christ which need to be formally rejected before becoming a Christian.

For many, a vow of nonviolence may be the sign of commitment to a new beginning to live as a Christian, rejecting the ways of violence and all dependence on weapons of violence. A vow of nonviolence may be a new form of renewal and confirmation into the Christian faith, a new "rite of initiation" like the baptismal promises. The vow may thrust the Christian into the way of Christ which is nonviolence, a way not often emphasized, preached or practiced. The vow of nonviolence is not an expression of one's unique calling within the Christian community but is an expression of one's calling to be a Christian. It may make explicit what godparents promised for a person at his or her baptism. It may indeed be an explicitation of one's baptismal commitment and thus a help to live the Christian life. It can be seen as a new baptismal commitment for Christians because, like the baptismal renewals, it is a rejection of Satan, that is, a rejection of nuclear weapons and all the violence of the world. It is instead an embrace of Christ, which means an embrace of peace-making solidarity with the poor and a lived commitment to evangelical nonviolence. The vow of nonviolence is the explicit rejection of the idols which have defended a person, such as Trident submarines or cruise missiles, and the embrace of the power of suffering love.

The vow of nonviolence makes explicit what is implicit in one's baptismal vow. One is not creating a new situation but merely professing to the world and specifically to the Christian community something which one has come to realize, that to be a Christian means to be nonviolent. The person may be receiving a new grace in the sense that he or she has discovered the existence of this grace in his or her Christian life and is now making a formal pledge of *acceptance.* This acceptance however demands an active response. The real power and commitment of the vow is in the fact that one can no longer say, "Oh, I didn't know this grace of nonviolence existed." Once one accepts the grace, he or she must live a new life *committed to the demands* of the gift.

The vow of nonviolence is the public recognition of something that has happened to a person, the recognition of who that person is. The person realizes that God has given him or her the grace of nonviolence, the desire to be nonviolent, and the will to be committed to the mission and way of nonviolence. Through the vow one accepts this great gift of God and may begin that life mission of loving nonviolence which God so desires. The vow of nonviolence is a response in faith in God; it is a gift from God, a gift of a lifetime that God has called one to accept and to live forever. The vowed life of nonviolence becomes a free choice that one accepts and chooses openly and wholeheartedly, over and over again, to the degree that one is open to God's grace. It can be the formal beginning of a lifetime of one's experiments in truth and love and can act as the shield in times of frustration, apparent hopelessness and futility. The vow of nonviolence is the public pledge and witness to the life ahead of witnessing to the reality of the reign of God which God is building and which already exists in one's heart and in the world.

It is thus a vow of allegiance to Jesus Christ, to his way of life—nonviolence—and to his reign of nonviolent love, a renewal of one's Christianity through nonviolence for the Christian.

The vow of nonviolence may then challenge a person out of the comfortable world of complacency into the dangerous, risky way of life which is nonviolence. It can thus be an instrument of renewal, a return to the matters of life, liberty and justice. Ultimately, a vow of nonviolence may lead to the constant conversion of one's heart toward a deeper nonviolence and union with God.

Thomas Merton wrote that nonviolence in deed is "nothing more than a living out of a nonviolence of the heart, an inner unity already experienced in prayer."[21] It is an understanding, loving attitude which perceives the world of human beings as a human family and thus it includes an active attitude of compassion and forgiveness in thought, word and deed toward all. It is based in the faith that each positive act and choice rooted in love and truth— *no matter how small*—will lead the human family to a greater conversion, transformation and redemption. One professes a vow of nonviolence because one is living out this experience of God's love *already* in one's heart, in prayer, in life. It is the full embrace of the nonviolent way of life and the free choice to pursue love and truth everywhere through loving and truthful decisions and actions.

It can mark the beginning of a life of experimentation in truth, the deepening of one's life of humble service toward the neediest and the poorest, and, indeed, perhaps the first step into real solidarity with the voiceless and the powerless, those who suffer the effects of violence. The vow of nonviolence is the pledge to seek constant conversion of heart through daily, continuous self-denial, active love and truth, and the promise to seek out complete abandonment and dependence on God by cultivating a nonviolent life in thoughts, words and deeds. The vow of nonviolence is the prayerful pledge made in freedom to do what is right no matter how hopeless a situation or life itself may appear. The willingness to serve, suffer, and deny oneself for the good of all, to overcome violence, hate and injustice with active love and the courageous insistence on truth is what the vow of nonviolence recognizes, captures and commits a person to forever.

It is a perpetual commitment to God, all humanity and oneself to strive to be nonviolent more and more in thought, word and deed at every moment in one's life. The bottom line or fundamental posture of the vow of nonviolence is simple: "*Recognizing* the violence in my heart, I will, to the best of my ability, *not* use violence on others or myself again, but will instead love others." One pledges not to harm others ever again, avoiding all the possible manifestations of violence, from inflicting physical injury or death, to participation in national or international violence, to verbal assault, harmful psychological manipulation, dishonesty, greed or hating another person in the privacy of one's heart. From this platform of abstaining from any use of violence, the vow offers a life of love in action, a commitment to love on all fronts. But even more, it becomes a pledge of resistance to injustice and violence, a pledge to overcome the evil of violence through active nonviolence, love and truth. The vow motivates one to resist and end violence anywhere and everywhere, for violence anywhere is violence committed against one's sisters or brothers, its victims and its victimizers, and therefore violence committed against oneself. The vow of nonviolence is a charism of the Spirit which sets one's heart and mind, body and soul on loving God in one's neighbor, in all of humanity. It places a person's awareness squarely into the world of violence and challenges him or her to love others, to be nonviolent.

The vow of nonviolence may best be professed in community, in the support of friends who are also trying to live nonviolent lives. One should prepare for the celebration of this commitment by studying nonviolence, reflecting on the experiences of some of its practitioners, experimenting in nonviolence, beginning anew the cultivation of a nonviolent heart through prayer and practice. A vow of nonviolence might include these ingredients: "I vow myself to perpetual nonviolence before God and the human family in my search for truth as I witness to the reign of God on earth through God's Spirit of reconciliation, love, justice and peace, in my own heart and mind, in all my relationships and in the world, following in the steps of Jesus Christ who shows the way with his life."

The vow of nonviolence is an instrument for the consideration of all those who want to reform their lives, all those who want to renew their faith in God, all those who are ready to accept the many graces of nonviolence. The vow can, as an instrument of God's grace, open up a new way of life for many people. It can thus be professed by anyone. The nonviolent life—in all its fullness and richness—can be adopted and embraced by anyone, by any human being who desires the nonviolent life and who hears the call of God to a deeper commitment of truth and love. Young people, Church leaders, all ministers, religious men and women, Catholics, priests, nuns, religious communities, all Christians, all those who seek truth and who long to serve suffering humanity and to follow the nonviolent life can consider making the life commitment of nonviolence by professing a vow. It can also be considered by married couples, as a help to becoming more nonviolent with each other and with their children, to fulfilling their commitment, and to being a sign of peace, hope, love and unity to their children and the world.

The vow of nonviolence is a real option for all who want to commit their lives to God and to humanity. It can be professed by those already working against systems of violence. Because it is a supportive, communal event, the vow may inspire a deeper search for the person and may inspire others into accepting and professing the nonviolent life, and help maintain that nonviolent spirit in the works of mercy and civil disobedience to injustice. It can be considered by peace activists who are seeking a renewal, and by community organizers, social workers and teachers.

The vow of nonviolence may be helpful to those who have spent many years in the work of resistance to nuclear weapons systems and who are sorely tempted to succumb to the spirit of violence in anger and frustration. True nonviolence and nonviolent direct action comes from a heartfelt spirit and releases truth through simple symbols, actions, which the whole world can understand and accept without being confused or turned off by any violent connotations.

After prayerful discernment, a vow of nonviolence can be especially helpful and meaningful to someone who has recently undergone a conversion, for example, a Christian convert. With the vow, people can pledge themselves to Christ's way of nonviolence in a way which recognizes the desire to follow the nonviolent Christ. The person who has made a career working for the military or in a nuclear weapons base may resign or leave his or her job in an effort to follow God's will. He or she may be called to profess a vow of nonviolence as a help to beginning his or her nonviolent life of radical Gospel living, in order to love and forgive unconditionally and to resist all injustice and oppression when family and friends do not understand one's efforts and beliefs. Those who are going to work in an area of persecution, violence and war, where people are suffering physically and dying unjust deaths, may decide to commit themselves by a vow to nonviolence before they go in an effort to stand firm and remain nonviolent in the face of such violence.

As a channel of grace, therefore, the vow can be a great support in one's life of nonviolence in a world addicted to violence, where nonviolent love is not often preached or accepted. It is an acceptance of the gift of nonviolence which God has given to a person and a public witnessing of this reality. In the life journey of nonviolence, one may discover that the vow may truly be a channel of grace which holds one to the commitment made with God to follow God in nonviolence. It may be the channel of God's strength and courage in the midst of the threat of violence or real injustice. A vow of nonviolence may be the channel of grace which helps some to remember God's covenant of love with us, to remember who we are and to remember how we can freely, wholeheartedly and humbly love others and hold steadfastly to the truth.

In the nuclear age, where so much has been lost with society's willingness to destroy itself, a vow may be the channel of needed encouragement and inspiration to stand firm to another way of life, to the way of nonviolence. But such a leap of faith into a way of life—ever-new, ever-changing, ever-open to the Spirit of God—will lead to consequences. These consequences and implications of such a life need to be faced squarely as one considers such a step.

6

Implications for the Life of Vowed Nonviolence

Less than one year after professing a vow of nonviolence, I was led to work in a soup kitchen and a night shelter in New York City, and then to live and work in a refugee camp for a few months in El Salvador, places where my convictions were tested and tried. The choice I made to embrace the nonviolent way of life influenced later decisions and my reactions in certain situations. The choice to become nonviolent, I soon discovered, will have consequences.

As a response to God's call and as a way of life, the vow of nonviolence will entail many implications for a person's life which over time will shape that life. A vow of nonviolence can lay the formal groundwork for a life of spontaneous, Spirit filled nonviolence which cannot be forced but which flows freely from one's being. The vow can help to continue setting the stage and forming the structure of one's attitudes so that a person may be open to allowing God's work of nonviolence to be done in his or her life. It can prepare a person and help that person to be ready to respond with creative nonviolence in any of the various situations in daily life and in every situation of provocative public nonviolence. In truth, the vow makes explicit what is implicit in one's heart, God's gift of Christian nonviolence. The vow is a sign of the reality of being "born again" in Jesus Christ through his nonviolence. This pledge to witness to God's great gift of Jesus Christ and the good news of his nonviolence will have specific implications and ramifications for a person. A look at the many characteristics involved in the life of vowed nonviolence will be helpful to demonstrate the very nature of the vowed nonviolent life and point out the ground on which one's creative nonviolent life will stand. These characteristics are surely inherent in the discipleship of every Christian as well. For the person vowed to nonviolence, they will be signs to the Christian community and the world of the gifts God has given that person and the gifts that God is continually offering to all human beings, God's children. All of these characteristics are gifts, grace built upon more grace, and cannot exist without God.

The vow commits oneself to the daily practice and pursuit of the spirit and actions of nonviolence. As I noted, because of the very definition of the vow, *agape* and truth will be at the forefront of one's new attitude of vowed nonviolence. The vow of nonviolence is a perpetual commitment to love other people with all of one's being. This love translates into an active willingness to suffer for others without retaliating and to serve others without expecting service in return. Nonviolent love is "not merely a negative state of harmlessness," explained Gandhi, "but a positive state of doing good even to the evil-doer. Nonviolence is active goodwill toward all life. It is pure love."[22]

Compassion is a good word to describe this fundamental attitude and lifestyle of *agape* which the vow of nonviolence entails. Compassion sums up the basis of the nonviolent attitude which one will cultivate in a vowed life. When Jesus spoke of being "compassionate" and "perfect" as God is "compassionate" and "perfect," he summed up the fullness of the nonviolent life which is pledged in the vow of nonviolence. Compassion calls for the recognition of the basic humanity in every person, oppressor or oppressed, the broken nature in everyone, and the fact that every human being is a child of God and thus related to every other human being as a brother or sister. The compassionate heart of nonviolence has a burning desire of love to help heal all those who are suffering from violence: be that hunger, war, murder, homelessness, the lack of freedom and dignity, or other forms of injustice.

This compassion invokes a life of service to others without expecting any reward. A better way to describe this service would be a perpetual desire to accompany those who are suffering under the structures of violence, and to aid and accompany them, as one's friends, in their effort and one's own effort to be free from violence. This vow commits one to spend one's life in loving service of others, especially those who suffer the brutal realities of violence. The vow of nonviolence is the pledge to spend one's life helping to relieve those who are suffering of their pain and misery, to serve suffering humanity through a concentrated nonviolent effort, to focus one's life on that purpose and that goal.

The vow then is a commitment to resist injustice, but without using violence and by being just and loving. At the heart of the definition of nonviolence is resistance to violence without using the means of violence. The nonviolent person who maintains heartfelt love for all people will renounce not only active aggression, but passive aggression, which is a more subtle and sometimes a more destructive form of hostility, as well. Employing the example of Jesus, Francis, Gandhi, Martin Luther King, Jr., Dorothy Day, and others, the vowed person uses creative energy to provoke change, to help others to see the injustice that is perpetuated and to suffer the violence inflicted on oneself in the process—if necessary—without returning that violence or retreating. This vow is a pledge in the pattern of Gandhi, who urged people "to lay down their lives for what they considered to be right."[23] Hatred, bitterness or revenge finds no place in this steadfast opposition to violence which always allows for reconciliation and the possibility of repentance and love. In actions of nonviolent resistance, the vowed resister says in effect, "I am so determined to right this injustice that I am willing to suffer to bring about change," instead of the more common and less effective reasoning which says, "I am so determined to right this injustice that I am going to make my opponent suffer for it."[24] The willingness to accept and absorb suffering and violence will often open the eyes of those inflicting the oppression to see what they are doing and to whom they are doing it—to fellow human beings.

In the nuclear age, faithfulness to one's vow of nonviolence will most likely lead to nonviolent acts of civil disobedience in order to influence governments to change their laws and the path of nuclear war which they have laid out. In the nuclear age and in time of war and injustice, some vowed to nonviolence may find themselves in prison for nonviolent insistence on justice. Serious preparations for acts of nonviolent, prayerful civil disobedience must always be made as well as the maintenance of a nonviolent attitude in prison. As one grows in the vowed nonviolent life, it will be hard to continue living without committing civil disobedience against governmental structures and nuclear weapons facilities. This will appear as the only right road to take—persistent actions on behalf of disarmament and justice and noncooperation with systemic injustice and violence until it has been converted into social programs that serve. Civil disobedience by people vowed to strict nonviolence will seek to end the abstraction of violence, to provoke the necessary tension between threatened violence and loving nonviolence, to force, through the power of suffering love, all people to see whom the structures of violence are killing, to end violence and to convert hardened hearts into love, truth and forgiveness. Nonviolent civil disobedience is part of the willingness to suffer in order to sting the conscience of the world and to shake people out of the spirit of violence which can so easily trap people. The vow of nonviolence frees one to break all barriers of violence by the power of love and truth.

Strict, meticulous adherence to truth and to searching for truth is fundamental for the life of nonviolence; it is part of the very definition of nonviolence, as discussed earlier. Gandhi called the nonviolent person not "one who abstains from violence," but a *satyagrahi,* "one who holds on to truth."[25] This faithfulness encompasses every choice and decision, every thought, word and deed. "All our activities should be centered in truth," Gandhi maintained. "Truth should be the very breath of our life." In the whole-hearted search for truth, only glimpses revealed in conscience may be attained. Yet these are sufficient for acting. One is willing to change and grow as truth is revealed. This requires the utmost respect for other individuals who cling to their glimpse of truth, and a persistent and focused effort to incarnate and realize truth in the present. Truth necessarily involves what is right, one's conscience, love, and nonviolence in all its ramifications. In order to pursue truth, the vow of nonviolence demands honesty. The person vowed to nonviolence strives therefore never to tell a lie or to participate in lies or self-deception.

Nonviolence and truth are not possible without a living belief in God, since God has created us and loved us first, and revealed God's essence in creation, salvation history and the Gospel. Since the person of nonviolence understands truth as God, God as truth-full, and seeks truth at every moment through a lively conscience, then this person must commit himself or herself to finding God's call and to focusing on God. Prayer is the instrument of this search. Gandhi once said, "My greatest weapon is mute prayer." The first and last act of the nonviolent person is prayer, and this prayer always leads to action. Daily prayer, contemplation, meditation, silence and solitude are necessary ingredients in the nonviolent life. Prayer demands time, solitude and faithful dedication in order for the fruit of love in nonviolent action to be true. God must be the motivating force in all efforts of nonviolence; indeed, without a relationship to God, the grace of God, the attitude of nonviolence cannot exist. "Prayer is most fundamentally a covenantal relationship with another person—God—and it partakes of all the risks, struggles, joys and darknesses that attach to any personal intimacy," writes John Kavanaugh.[26] Daily discernment on how to act out or to respond to God's grace of nonviolence is needed to open one's heart and mind to God's love and God's suggestions. God whispers his desires for active nonviolence in the listening posture and daily dialogue of love that is prayer. Some have referred to this as listening to the "inner still voice" within each that provokes love and nonviolence. Any nonviolent action must be a response to God's action in one's life. In order to be able to respond to God, the vowed person of nonviolence needs to experience and love God personally as lover, friend, confidant and parent, not merely to know *about* God. In fact, to profess the vow of nonviolence, one will have experienced the reality of God's love already and recognized God's gift of love to oneself. This intimate awareness of the love of God can grow in the building of the lifelong intense relationship that is founded in daily prayer. Besides the daily private prayer of solitude, communal worship and regular reflection and examination of one's life are also necessary roots for the nonviolent life.

Prayer begins from a confession of sin and includes petitions for all those classified as enemies in order to bring about greater reconciliation. Penance, fasting, and spiritual asceticism are fundamental regular requirements of prayer for the vowed life of nonviolence. From prayer, a person is able to act in love for those formally considered enemies. Implicit in the prayer and faith life of the person vowed to nonviolence is the total trust in God and a state of complete dependence on God. To be nonviolent presumes a commitment to be faithful in prayer with God, even though one is weak and sinful. Prayerful communication in the presence of God demands faith; faith demands prayer in order to exist, survive and grow. The nonviolent attitude can only mature through the continual recognition of one's identity as a child of God which happens in prayer when the limits of one's being are revealed before God. Vowing nonviolence is the commitment to God, to working for world reconciliation in whatever capacity one is capable of, but most basically to praying daily for reconciliation, reorientation to God and unity among all people. This prayer pleads for one's conversion of heart and then for the conversion of hearts among all people.

The vow of nonviolence will mean a life of prayer and contemplation that goes hand in hand with the action of our nonviolent love. By constantly opening up our lives more and more to God in a prayerful, peaceful way, by becoming more open and disposed to the grace of God, by cooperating with the grace of God, what we do will hopefully originate from God and be done with a peace in the very depths of our beings. With this desire, God will lead us, use us, and do with us what he wants.

Ultimately, the person vowed to nonviolence is not seeking or worshiping nonviolence, but trying to imitate God and worship God who is and always will be nonviolent. The vowed nonviolent life is the lived search for God in one's life and in the world. When one seeks the truth with one's whole mind, heart, strength, soul, will, understanding and memory, when one acts on behalf of and in search of the truth at every moment of one's existence, God is found and continually found. The search for truth leads to trust in God for insights into himself. Total trust in God opens one's eyes and mind to see truth in all life situations. The more one trusts in God, the more one hands over one's whole existence, life, hopes, desires, prayers and works to God, and the more one will discover, live, and breathe truth in complete abandonment.

The search for truth, which can begin with a vow of nonviolence, goes beyond all religious and secular loyalties to define the real allegiance to God. Douglass states: "A person knows truth as relative, but if he/she worships that relative truth and deepens in it, he/she is certain to attain Absolute Truth."[27] This total, all-encompassing pursuit of truth or God is at the heart of the person of nonviolent suffering love. The vowed person will say with Gandhi, who wrote in his *Autobiography:* "I have not yet found God but I am seeking after God. I am prepared to sacrifice things dearest to me in pursuit of this quest. Even if that sacrifice demanded be my very life, I hope I may be prepared to give it. . . . God alone is real and all else is unreal."[28]

Connected with this search for truth is the sharing of found truth with others. In the adoption of what one sees as truth, the person of vowed nonviolence will humbly and boldly witness to others what is right and true, for example, to nonviolence. With respect, concern and love for people, one committed to truth must stand up publicly and object to any doctrine, structure, obstruction or denial that blasphemes truth, even when it is dangerous, scandalous and risky to do so. Truth pursued and proclaimed in a spirit of love and openness is always victorious and always leads a person to greater freedom.

A deep trust in God and a commitment to love and truth through a vow of nonviolence will allow for a greater freedom from fear, a great obstacle to love and a root cause of violence. Fearlessness, when one is not afraid of anyone or anything because no one/nothing has power over oneself, except God, is a grace that is received and cultivated throughout one's life of nonviolence. Many fears plague humanity, including fear of rejection, abandonment, denial, betrayal, loneliness, embarrassment, imprisonment, pain, torture, or having one's pride or self-worth challenged. All of these fears can kill the soul in one way or another.

But the fear of death may be perhaps the greatest underlying fear. A life of perpetual nonviolence requires such great faith, trust and dependence in God that all fears vanish, including the fear of death. Death is perceived no longer as an unknown threat but the fuller entrance into the reign of truth, love, reconciliation and God. Living free from the fear of death means living in acceptance of one's death at any moment as the joyful grace of union with God. Living each day in the present moment, as if it were one's last day on earth, will help toward greater honesty, love, faith and fearlessness and inner peace so characteristic of the nonviolent life. The vow of nonviolence is the pledge to accept the grace of one's death, one's passage into eternity without fear and with joy, so that if through one's active nonviolence one faces the possibility of a violent death, one will be ready to hand over one's life in a spirit of love and nonviolence to God and maintain a spirit of nonviolence and forgiveness toward others. In the face of violence, the person vowed to nonviolence can be faithful to the vow by remaining calm and unafraid, maintaining dialogue and eye contact if necessary, and a composure of love and truth that is rooted in one's faith identity. In the life of vowed nonviolence, a person is encouraged to name one's fears, to put them behind, and to act against them without any fear. Trust in God enables the courageous step to break beyond fear, to believe that God supports and defines the actions of life. Faith in God's boundless love and steadfast loyalty to truth open new channels of freedom, self-respect and security in God's love so that nothing—no fear—can bind one down. Freedom from all worries and anxieties is also a necessary choice and grace along the path of the nonviolent life. Prayer and the ensuing active nonviolence should not be grounded in an anxious, nervous, worried spirit but always grounded in an inner peace of trust, acceptance, faith and dependence on God.

Courage, the spirit of love and truth based in fearlessness and a strong faith and trust in God, is needed in this vowed life to stand up and resist injustice and violence everywhere through nonviolence and to live out the nonviolent life. In a tense situation or conflict where physical violence may appear imminent, a nonthreatening, nonintimidating response is always possible. Courage is the strength to give away what is asked of oneself and more, the strength not to give in to violence or submit to fear, intimidation or oppression, and the strength to remain standing firm in one's nonviolence and one's grasp of truth and justice. Through self-discipline and prayer, courage enables one to maintain a disarming attitude of friendship even in the face of violence which one has revealed or provoked by uncovering the truth. By refusing to frighten, intimidate or threaten another, the person vowed to nonviolence hopes to draw forth the good that is in everyone. The effort seeks to free those who partake in acts of injustice and violence by demonstrating to them that any act of hostility they intend is inconsistent with the kind of person they truly wish to be. In the courageous act of befriending the other's better nature, one always maintains that "even the most brutal and brutalized have some spark of decency" in their shared humanity that can be touched.[29]

While God can empower a person through vowed nonviolence to love and to act fearlessly, God will also invite, through vowed nonviolence, a choice of lifestyle and a commitment of solidarity: to side with the powerless and to adopt their powerlessness. Nonviolence requires one to renounce all coercive power over another in this life, to accompany those who have no control over their lives, and to place all control over one's life into the powerful hands of God. To be nonviolent in today's world is to shun all coercive power, to have nothing to do with violent power, and to let the power of God act instead through one's powerlessness. Vulnerability and powerlessness happen when security and worldly defense through violence, intimidation, control, and dependence on possessions are abandoned, and one's security is achieved and found only in God, in the community of God's people. The reality of the vow of nonviolence will be incarnated in one's life when the vowed person embraces a life of voluntary poverty and non-possession, and lives in solidarity with those who have no choice in the matter—the poor, the powerless, the voiceless, the hungry, the homeless. The vow of nonviolence is a commitment to enter the world of the poor, the outcasts, the despised, and to join in their state as fully as possible. It is the scandalous, risky, dangerous act of giving up the values of the Western world and entering into lifelong relationships and friendships with those who have nothing and who suffer the injustice of the world. It means accompanying them in their suffering and powerlessness and thus offering hope to them. Living simply with the poor is a necessity of the nonviolent life and the ultimate expression and witness of nonviolence. The bold proclamation and the good news of nonviolence can best be heard not just in prophetic words and a wealthy lifestyle, but in the powerful witness and example of one's very life, in the life of voluntary poverty and solidarity with the poor, the oppressed and the voiceless.

To reject violence at its roots demands renunciation of all possessions and a life of voluntary poverty shared with the poor and oppressed. Involuntary poverty or destitution is one of the worst forms of violence; owning possessions which one does not need means owning possessions that belong to others and will create destitution. Chosen voluntary poverty lived among those who had no choice in the matter is necessary in order for one not to be a part of the unjust economic structures which oppress and kill people, but so that one can share a life of suffering under oppression and the necessary struggle for nonviolent liberation. Once the life of simplicity and solidarity with the poor is embraced, one can maintain a spirit of hospitality, the willingness to welcome anyone into one's heart and to share one's spirit and world with others. Through chosen poverty and an attitude of love, God will then work through chosen nonviolence to empower his poor people and to liberate them to the fullness of life.

In this position, one can recognize his or her own weaknesses, accept them, and rely on God for everything. Making oneself vulnerable and powerless does not mean becoming passive, but refusing to resort to the false security and defense which is violence, intimidation or control over others. By living a life of actual poverty, letting go of all possessions and privileges and clinging to nothing as one's own, the nonviolent person can freely open himself or herself to others "with the faithful expectation that strength will manifest itself in shared weakness, thus creating a real community of the weak who are rich in God's power."[30] Powerlessness is ultimately the letting go of any sense of accomplishment or concern for effectiveness, and instead a living out of what is right and just and trusting in God to bring about victorious reconciliation. When nonviolence appears to bring about only failure, frustration, incompleteness, discomfort, dissatisfaction and a sense of loss, one may be approaching greater and necessary solidarity with the poor and the powerless. Perseverance in doing what is right and true and abandonment of control are still necessary. Shared powerlessness in community with the poor and among those who have embraced poverty and nonviolence helps to reveal shared mortality and shared humanity among people and thus can spark a common respect and dignity—reconciliation—among people. The vow of nonviolence will mean living out of an emptiness, and knowing that everything you do, every day, no matter how small and how apparently insignificant, if done in love and in truth, can tap into the love of God and be used by God to help others, to help bring peace to others. Greed, the desire for possessions, and the protection of one's possessions which is part of it, lies at the heart of all violence. Actual poverty must be embraced in freedom and self-emptying love. The choice for voluntary poverty, made in freedom and self-emptying love, is the choice for holiness and truth, the choice to imitate God. Because the poor are less pretentious, more open and dependent on God due to the marginalization and oppression they suffer, and because they have the power to disarm the greatest fears, nonviolence invites everyone to live with, for and like the poor in a true spirit of love.

In this life of powerlessness, voluntary poverty, and empowerment through nonviolence, one is also called to chastity as a way of life, whether as a single person or a married person or as a consecrated celibate. The vow of nonviolence is a pledge to a deeper reverence for the gift of human sexuality and the dignity of every human being and away from possible violent attitudes. In the daily living of the vow of nonviolence, one tries to cultivate and choose purity of heart, which is purity in body, mind, soul, and spirit. Nonviolence in chastity will free a person to a deeper, more complete life of love, truth and faith in God.

Linked to this life of powerlessness, poverty and purity of heart is the life of true humility: freedom from pride, ambition and seeking honor. Our cooperation with God's grace through chosen poverty, powerlessness and humility will mean letting go of our pride and ambition and our desires to become powerful and well-known, and instead entering into the reality, the hidden, humble life of the poor. The truly humble heart of the person vowed to nonviolence does not partake in any competition or comparison but rests in a basic trust of other people. Nonviolence demands an awareness "of how risky it is to claim to be making the truth known. . . . The most effective peacemakers," writes Jim Wallis, "are those who have experienced the healing of their own fears."[31] Active nonviolence must always reflect this spirit of contrition, humility and invitation. The nonviolent quest is an effort to become humbler still by abandoning all self-interest, moment by moment, by understanding one's limitations, mistakes and sinfulness through honest self-examination, by a deeper understanding of one's humanity and identity, and by accepting the reign of God in one's life. A humble spirit never forgets one's basic equality with all other human beings and rejects arrogance or superiority. True humility is marked by a spirit of gratitude to God and gentleness. The humble nonviolent person always trusts others by being inclusive and open toward all people and accepts the humiliation brought on by the scandal of nonviolence without resorting to violence but with renewed prayer and active nonviolence. Competition cannot be practiced and must be avoided because in the end it does not promote unqualified reconciliation but egotism, domination, power, control and, ultimately, violence. Rooted in envy and pride, it is one of the cornerstones of violence and can be a means to violence.

False humility does not characterize the vowed nonviolent life. One cannot dismiss any effort to overcome injustice through active love because one is "too humble to do anything or too sinful to act." Humility demands that one act with compassion despite one's sinfulness and weaknesses because the focus is on God's leadership. Any effort to use one's vow of nonviolence to prove one's dedication or point to one's importance or holiness contradicts the very essence of the vow. Nonviolence as true humility will overcome a poor self-image, an arrogant, self-righteous feeling of superiority, or the manipulative spirit that seeks approval and affirmation at every turn.[32] The vowed nonviolent person always endeavors to abandon all pride, honor, power and glory for a life of dependency on God, suffering love, simplicity and service.

Jim Wallis points to the strict commitment to love and humility which the vowed nonviolent person must maintain when he writes about the careful, discerning spirit that is needed in all nonviolent action:

> Whenever our protest becomes an effort to "prove ourselves," we are in serious danger. Our best actions are

those which admit our complicity in the evil we protest and are marked by a spirit of genuine repentance and humility. Our worst actions are those which seek to demonstrate our own righteousness, our purity, our freedom from complicity. When our pride overtakes our protest, we may simply be repeating, in political form, the self-righteous judgment of the fundamentalists—"I'm saved, and you're not." . . . Although our actions we undertake will never substitute for grace, they can indeed be witnesses of God's grace. Since they lack the capacity to justify us, a better purpose for our actions would be to bear faithful witness.[33]

Mercy, the spirit of unconditional forgiveness, is the last fundamental mark of the life of vowed nonviolence. Our attitude of mercy will enable us to forgive others for the smallest deeds that have hurt us, as well as allow us to forgive those who would kill our friends or our family members or us. This mercy is so pure it seeks to abolish any anger, judgment, cynicism, bitterness, condemnation or hatred in one's heart, thought, words or deeds by replacing them with endless gentleness toward oneself, others and God. The nonviolent person cultivates a spirit of gratitude and patient perseverance and avoids judging or condemning others. The vow of nonviolence will then be a promise not to judge others and not to condemn others. Being merciful toward others, that is, living out of a stance of perpetual forgiveness toward every human being, and still remaining faithful to the truth, can invite greater freedom, affirmation, friendship and reconciliation. By withdrawing any sign of hostility or threat, a merciful attitude always promotes reconciliation.

"It has always been a mystery to me how people can feel themselves honored by the humiliation of their fellow human beings," Gandhi wrote in his autobiography.[34] Any humiliating stance or structure breaks down the human family and causes resentment, anger, hatred and violence. A vow of nonviolence invites a person to be freed from humiliating others which is oppression. Rather than humiliate others, the person vowed to nonviolence must edify other people through mercy and love and helping others fulfill their true vocations as children of God.

The vow of nonviolence is a pledge to forgive every human being for the sinful thought, word, or deed which has been committed. In this spirit of forgiveness, the vowed person of nonviolence does not seek justice as it is commonly perceived. Punishment and retribution are never demanded or asked. Blanket forgiveness is always given. Instead of achieving justice by punishing oppressors, the vowed nonviolent person forgives oppressors and invites a change of heart and life, a new reconciliation between peoples.

To do this, the person of nonviolence must become free from anger. Anger directed toward others or oneself is one more participation in the spirit of violence which can creep into one's life and eat away at the spirit of love, thus leaving an empty shell of bitterness. Anger toward others offends God and does not reflect God; God does not harbor anger, but mercy. The vowed nonviolent person will never harbor anger toward others but choose instead to suffer away the anger of the opponent, and all the while refuse to submit to their anger or retaliate with the same anger and violence. One cannot be nonviolent—loving and compassionate—toward others if one is angry at them. Anger must be acknowledged, accepted as part of one's sinful state, dealt with and rejected through prayer and penance in order to be converted into nonviolent loving forgiveness. Anger against injustice and violence, when not directed at people but at the works of evil, can be channeled to motivate a person to respond with nonviolent resistance. Anger toward injustice can be acted on and dealt with in a non-violent way. This nonviolent resistance must be grounded in mercy toward others and envision a merciful goal—equality for all, freedom from sin as far as possible, and reconciliation.

If the person vowed to nonviolence is ever in a threatening situation or about to be harmed, or if he or she is present as someone is harming another person, then that person will try to respond with immediate loving resistance, based in a living faith in God who will act through this nonviolent spirit. Personal nonviolence extends even to such dramatic instances and demands courageous and active responses of love and trust in God. The vowed nonviolent person will intervene and do everything possible short of violence to stop any threat of violence or actual violence. The nonviolent person who is attacked will give away any material goods that are asked for, but will never give in to the violence nor submit to injustice, fear, intimidation and oppression. He or she will seek to maintain a posture of love, mercy and forgiveness and seek to disarm others with an open hand of friendship in an effort to free others from anger, violence and the sick need to oppress others.

Besides trusting in God to act when God's will is obeyed, the person of vowed nonviolence trusts in other people as human beings who share a basic goodness that can be called forth. Mutual trust characterizes the friendship that is sought and built. To reach mutual trust, unilateral trust in another person's basic goodness and humanity is necessary at every occasion. Personal nonviolence opens the way to complete trust in other people on each and every occasion. Such a trust in others will encourage greater trust in God, greater freedom, openness and honesty.

Through conscious effort, discipline and practice, non-violent love can become a reflex response applied in all relationships and encounters and can shape one's life work of active nonviolent resistance and witness.[35] Discernment, repentance, regular study, dialogue, careful reading of the times and the work of God, faithful contemplation, letting go of one's own plans and letting God's Spirit lead the way will lead to a faithful life of the way of nonviolence. Non-cooperation with consumerism and any forms of entertainment that support or promote violence can be adopted so that active nonviolence will become one's lifework. Ascetical practices and self-denial will help one to become more nonviolent to others and toward oneself. A humble attitude, free from all self-righteousness and rooted in God's love, is a key to unlocking the door to a life of vowed non-violence. One will continually act against egocentric motives and seek only to do the will of God. It is a life of steadfastness, faithfulness to God and the Gospel vision, no matter how confusing or ineffective the road may seem. Such a commitment, if faithful and open to God's Spirit, will be marked by a spontaneous joy and a deep reverence for all life.

The grace of God channeled through the vow of non-violence, in summary, has many real, hard and demanding implications for one's life if its challenge is to be met and fulfilled, if one is faithful to it. The vow of nonviolence is a perpetual pledge of militant nonviolence—unconditional love, forgiveness and mercy toward all. This active love is rooted in the pursuit of truth which requires justice for all. This militant nonviolence demands both love and truth at the same time; one cannot exist without the other. The vow is a perpetual commitment not to be violent, which includes avoiding harming another person or others, hating others, or lying; it is also a perpetual commitment to active love, *agape* and truth. The vow pledges heart, mind, soul and body on a lifelong, disciplined love and search for God in one's neighbor. Vowed nonviolence not only renounces all violence but celebrates complete commitment, the continued, free and active choice for God, truth and love, and always honors the gift of life in all its fullness. Vowed nonviolence is the pledge not to spend one's life in participating in the world of violence, in the pursuit of money, fame, honor, or power and so to die, but to lose oneself, to die to oneself in pursuit of love and truth and so to find life. Faith, fearlessness, powerlessness, voluntary poverty, humility, mercy and forgiveness—coupled with adamant nonviolent resistance to injustice—characterize this twofold pledge of love and truth.

Through the vow of nonviolence, God may create "soldiers of nonviolence," practitioners of militant nonviolence or truth-seekers who are disciplined in every thought, word and deed to respond with and initiate active nonviolence. Beginning in one's heart, this vowed nonviolence extends to all of humanity. It is a perpetual attitude and way of life and encompasses one's whole being. The vowed nonviolent person will be free to suffer and to die in the struggle for love and truth, but never to kill or to harm anyone. The new life of vowed nonviolence is a life spent at the service of suffering humanity which has become victimized by violence. It is the struggle to change the violence of suffering into redemptive love, a love which is painful and costly yet ultimately victorious and God-like. The life of vowed nonviolence is a life of freedom that reveals the fruits of the Holy Spirit: love, peace, joy, patience, kindness, goodness, faithfulness, gentleness, and self-control or chastity.

By pledging the vow, a person prays, "Yes, I want to try to practice nonviolence in the search for truth even though I am sinful, weak, broken and usually not very help-ful . . . but take me, God, take my good desires and do with me what you will." The vow is the pledge to become a saint, to become a lover of God, to accept the grace of God's non-violence in one's life, to strive for radical holiness through the means of justice and nonviolent love, and to witness to the gift of nonviolence and disarmament which God has given. It is the start of a life of experimenting in truth, of seeking to learn the truth. In the process of learning the truth, the vowed person will try to live truthfully, sponta-neously acting out and loving the truth through nonvio-lence, no matter what the cost, no matter what the danger. The life of vowed nonviolence continually asks one ques-tion and responds to whatever answer is discovered: "What does God want me to do? What does God want me to do right now for peace, for truth, for love, for the human fam-ily, for God right at this moment and for all moments in my life, especially in light of the gift of nonviolence which God has given me?" The answer will always take some form of love, love that is a risk and a challenge, love that is dangerous, hard and sacrificial. The vowed life of question-ing and answering God's will involves simply being person-ally disarmed and disarming, ready to do what God requests, at every turn, for the suffering human family which God loves so much.

7

The High Price of Nonviolent Love

Christians who embrace nonviolence often claim that all Christians, ultimately all human beings, are called to be nonviolent. Some then object that a vow of nonviolence will only limit its practice to a select few and create tensions by creating a new "elitism." Others claim that Christians cannot rightfully vow themselves to only one tradition in Church ethical teaching. Still others argue that Jesus forbade the profession of vows when he commanded his followers not to swear at all. The answers to these and other questions can shed further light on the reasons and implications of vowed nonviolence.

In discussions about vowed nonviolence, the question has often been asked, "But aren't all Christians called to be nonviolent?" If a select few profess themselves to nonviolence, it is argued, then others will begin to believe that nonviolence is just for the professed, for an "elite" few who take a vow and not for all Christians. There is no need to profess a vow of nonviolence, it is said, because it is part of the very definition of being a Christian. Every Christian is committed to Christ's nonviolence in his or her baptism. A vow of nonviolence will simply promote the view that nonviolence is just for some Christians, a charism to one group not given to every member of the body of Christ. People will begin to accept this error through believing that not every Christian is called to be nonviolent. The fear is that a vow of nonviolence will encourage those who do not profess it to ease their consciences. If nonviolence is a moral imperative for every Christian, critics argue, then vowed nonviolence will limit its full practice among all.

I have come to believe that loving, humble nonviolence is indeed a moral imperative for every Christian. Following Jesus in today's world means allowing God to disarm one's heart and practicing public, creative nonviolence toward one and all.

But Christian churches have a long and sinful history which our time and age may help to change by renewing our call to nonviolence. Historical research has shown that for the first three centuries, the Christian community was indeed pacifist. No Christian author at that time wrote of the Christian's duty to participate in war or in the military. It was taken for granted that Christians did not kill and would not kill or participate in the military forces. "From the end of the New Testament period to the decade A.D. 170–180," writes Roland Bainton, "there is no evidence whatever of Christians in the army. . . . From then on the references to Christian soldiers increase."[36] From that point until the time of Constantine, many Christian writers made explicit condemnations of military service. "The early Christians took Jesus at his word, and understood his inculcations of gentleness and non-resistance in their literal sense," explained C. John Cadoux. "They closely identified their religion with peace; they strongly condemned war for the bloodshed which it involved; they appropriated to themselves the Old Testament prophecy which foretold the transformation of the weapons of war into the implements of agriculture; they declared that it was their policy to return good for evil and to conquer evil with good."[37] The early Christians understood the nonviolence of Jesus as imperative for themselves and thus tried to live it out.

Through this "meekness" and "gentleness," the original
followers formed a nonviolent community which acknowledged the Lordship of Christ and saw the regular arrest,
imprisonment and martyrdom of its members. By the time
Emperor Constantine officially recognized Christianity as
the religion of the empire in the early fourth century, the
nonviolent tradition of the Church began to pass into the
monasteries, where it was reserved for those "called to perfection."[38] With the development of the just war tradition
and the holy war tradition, radical nonviolence began to
disappear as a public witness of the Church.

As Jim Wallis has explained, the Church needs to
return to the grace of witnessing to the world about another
way of life which is following Jesus Christ in his way of
nonviolence. Wallis has written at length about the role of
the Christian and the role of the Church in today's world:

> A Christian is more than someone who wants to
> change things; a Christian is someone who is being
> changed. Christian radicalism is not a strategy but the
> result of transformation. The process of change begins
> as we give ourselves over to Christ. It involves giving
> up our right to ourselves and depending upon God.
> The key to the kingdom is faithfulness in following
> Christ daily. Therefore, the Christian style of life is not
> an objective but a consequence of obedience and wit-
> ness. The Christian lifestyle is a life of testimony. . . .
> The church's most serious shortcoming stems from its
> failure to *be* what the church has been called to be,
> from failing to structure its life and action as that new
> community created by the work of Christ and empow-
> ered by the Holy Spirit to be a new social reality, a liv-
> ing testimony to the presence of the kingdom of God
> in the world. . . . Basic and primary to the task of Chris-
> tians today is to recover the biblical vision of the

church as the people of God—a new social reality in
the midst of the life of the world.[39]

It is this return to the reality of the kingdom of God to
which the Church must witness and proclaim to the world.
With the vow of nonviolence, no one is initiating a new
gnosticism, a new branch of belief where we claim we have
all the answers and the only way to God. Nor is this the
beginning of a new elitist group. Rather, in vowed nonviolence, some Christians are finding an aid to further renewal
and empowerment in their lives of faith and justice.

For some, a vow of nonviolence may be an instrument
of God which allows the Spirit to breathe new life into the
world today and encourages Christians to witness to the
world about God's kingdom. Vowed nonviolence may stir
the Spirit of love in us to act in this nuclear age, in all new
zealous ways, and thus spark greater conversion and
renewal. If some vow themselves to Gospel nonviolence,
and remain faithful to its practice, they may find themselves now open to newer graces and gifts from the Holy
Spirit which they had not imagined. Special vows of nonviolence may be needed in our day and age for Christians
to commit themselves to a more faithful, active following
of Jesus Christ. It may help make the implicit nonviolence
of Christianity explicit in the lifestyles, practices and
acts of Christians. The vow may inspire Christians to a
greater, zealous love and truth-seeking so necessary for
overcoming systemic evil in today's world. Vowed nonviolence may encourage the reteaching and evangelization of
the Christian way of nonviolence. Christians may become
more motivated to be more active and zealous in pursuit
of the kingdom of God on earth and to be better centered
in their hearts on God and God's Spirit. Vowed nonviolence may help spread the heart of the Christian message,

that we are all God's children, and give life, purpose, integrity and relevance to our Christianity which has become lukewarm.

Perhaps vowed nonviolent Christians will be the turn which takes the Church and more Church members down the path that marked the age of martyrs after the resurrection of Jesus. The vow of nonviolence, as a channel of grace and an instrument for witnessing to God's disarmament of the Christian community, may free Christians to break loose from the shackles of apathy and societal pressure to support systemic violence. It may free Christians to live the Gospel message of Jesus in their hearts, to make real choices on behalf of the poor and the marginalized no matter what the consequences, to become poor and marginalized themselves like Jesus. It may provide Christians with the strength and the courage to act out their faith in the nuclear age *without fear* of the threat or the use of violence or death. It may help Christians to incarnate the Word which teaches us that the way to right wrongs is to take on suffering, not inflict it. Vowed nonviolence may be appropriate at this point in history as a good step for the Christian community's pilgrimage into the kingdom of God. It may help us to reset our sights on God and to be more faithful to the slow building of the kingdom which has many more years of constructive conversion ahead. It may help keep us stay awake, alert, and more faithful in a time of violence.

Because it is a pledge of acceptance of God's nonviolence and a witness to the world, a vow of nonviolence may simply encourage people not to give up the struggle of love, voluntary suffering and steadfast truth. It may help those Christians working in especially violent areas or situations of "abstracted" systemic violence who are trying to overcome violence with nonviolence but are finding the long commitment difficult, draining and impossible. It may help deepen one's spiritual and actual commitment and heal the burnt out, embittered or despairing person.

The vow of nonviolence is especially fitting and proper when seen in the light of Christian tradition. The possibility of Christians vowing themselves to Gospel nonviolence and universal suffering love continues the good tradition in Church history of public, religious vows and private devotional vows which were the cause of great renewal at times in the Church's history. The commitment made by Francis and his followers in the thirteenth century, for example, to Gospel poverty breathed a whole new Spirit and way of life into Christianity which had been forgotten. Similarly, vows of nonviolence may breathe new life into the Church in this nuclear age. It can be professed by anyone who longs to be more faithful to the way of love.

Those who do not accept Christian nonviolence but do accept the just war theory may raise another objection: "Can Christians rightfully vow themselves to only one tradition in Christian ethical teaching?" The question arises from a defense of the just war theory. As we have discussed, nonviolence is a way of life open to all people. It is a way of life for all Christians. Even the just war theory shares the common presumption against the use of force as a means of settling disputes. However, because of the realities of the nuclear age, the just war theory is no longer applicable. The acceptance of deterrence as a national policy is no longer acceptable, and Christians are beginning to rise to a new level of understanding and awareness. Christians are beginning to see God's reign and to accept the consequences of believing in God and acting in that belief.

Some object to the profession of any kind of vow, argu-

ing that Jesus was against vows. They cite the fourth antith-
esis of the Sermon on the Mount:

> You have learned how it was said to our ancestors: You
> must not break your oath, but must fulfill your oaths
> to the Lord. But I say this to you: do not swear at all,
> either by heaven, since that is God's throne; or by the
> earth, since that is his footstool; or by Jerusalem, since
> that is the city of the great king. Do not swear by your
> own head either, since you cannot turn a single hair
> white or black. All you need say is "Yes" if you mean
> yes, "No" if you mean no; anything more than this
> comes from the evil one (Mt 5:33–37).

This text teaches people not to take oaths or to swear
at all. This command of Jesus is an effort to avoid legalism,
the loss of the Spirit of God, and to encourage people only
to speak the truth if they wish to follow him. At the heart
of this pericope is the teaching that commitment to God's
invitation is not to be lived out of coercion or fear of punishment, but in a Spirit of Truth. Too often promises or
vows are conceived as exterior laws to which we submit.
Thus, however good the content of the vow, the vow itself
remains exterior to us. This has naturally led, both in theory and in practice, to a coercive understanding of vows,
whereby vows were to be enforced and mistakes punished.
In an oath, God is called upon to witness to a truth, and
thus to enforce through coercion any error. Vows are different, as we discussed earlier. They are professed to God
and one another as expressions of our deepest desires to be
the kind of persons we are and are called to be. Jesus
teaches here that we cannot claim God as a witness or control God for our own purposes. Vows are public recogni-
tions of what God has already done and the pledge of
acceptance of and cooperation with this grace of God. They

are not efforts to control God. Christians have been making promises since the days of Christ, in their baptisms and in their baptismal renewals. These promises expressed the longing of the catechumen and the Christian to be a new person in Christ, to continue to receive and live out of the new life to which God had called them. A sweeping rejection of all solemn promises to God, of vows, mistakes the proper understanding of a vow, tends to confuse a vow with an oath (where God is portrayed as an external "enforcer"), and runs in sharp contrast to one of the most ancient practices of the Church. Vows are not oaths, nor are they pledges to a narrow-minded ideology which limits a person. Vows are a mediation to a fuller life, a help toward becoming more human. They are life-giving channels of grace into a life of faith.

In light of these words of Jesus, a vow, such as a vow of nonviolence, is indeed a "Yes" to what God is doing in one's life. It is the public acceptance of the gift of nonviolence which God has given to a person; it is saying "Yes" to God and meaning it with all one's heart and soul. When one professes perpetual nonviolence in a vow, one is saying "Yes" to Jesus and his call to be nonviolent like him. It is the declaration that one will mean "Yes," that one will take seriously the lifelong commitment of loving, humble, active nonviolence in following Jesus. The "Yes" to God in vowed nonviolence differs from oaths or military vows. Unlike the presidential oath taken under God's name to protect, defend and uphold the Constitution of the United States, unlike any military oath or governmental oath (and unlike Herod's oath to his daughter to give her whatever she wanted), the vow of nonviolence claims the search for truth through the flexible, discernible guidance of the Holy Spirit and is professed to the living God in the hopes of imitating God's unconditional love. The vow pleads, "Yes,

I want to try to practice Gospel nonviolence in the search for the truth even though I am sinful, weak, broken and usually not very helpful ... but take me, God, take my good desires and do with me what you will." It is the promise to accept the grace of nonviolence which God is giving to a person, not any kind of swearing. It is a response to an invitation from God, not a legalistic practice. It is a *kenosis,* an emptying of oneself into the nonviolent journey to God which God has initiated, to a radical dependence and obedience to God, and to the vision of the disarmed human family which God has revealed to that person. It is lived out in freedom, not under coercion. We know that Jesus said "Yes" to God's invitation to be poor, chaste and nonviolent and was thus always obedient to the will of God. In order to follow Jesus in perpetual poverty, chastity, nonviolence and obedience to the will of God, Christians need to stand up at many times throughout their lives and say "Yes" to God's invitation. A vow of nonviolence is one way of doing this.

Some people may say that Christians should not profess vows of nonviolence because the Pharisees of Jesus' day professed vows similar to nonviolence and Jesus was so opposed to the legalism and rigidity which they may have settled into. However, the Pharisees were not pledged to nonviolence as the strict adherence to truth and love, the willingness to suffer violence without retaliating in order to overcome evil and the willingness to serve others without reciprocation. Some Pharisees, like most people of their day, practiced a submission to the governments of their day in the hopes that a messiah would come and bring judgment and become their earthly king, adopting the way of power and violence used in the world. Such practice trapped them and most others into the complicity of enjoying the benefits of violence and oppression. As with most people of their day, they were supporters of the systemic violence, injustice and oppression of their day. The passivism of the Pharisees lacked the scandal, the spontaneity, and the risky, dangerous insistence on truth and love which marks the nonviolence that stands up to oppression and injustice. Such passivity and complicity is not unlike those who today support, through their financial resources, apathy or willingness, the systemic violence, the laws and the oppression which harm people and cause us to forget that we are brothers and sisters—such as capital punishment, consumerism, torture, nuclear weapons and war. Vowed active nonviolence is revolutionary love and insistence on real justice and truth. It is neither passive nor violent in force; it is characterized by the acceptance of suffering in order to change evil into good.

Some charge that a vow of nonviolence is a mistake because "nonviolence does not work." Because Gospel nonviolence is so rarely demonstrated in society, many still do not understand the great power of love and truth involved in cooperation with grace. Active nonviolence always leads to further reconciliation, yet we may not see the results ourselves. It must be remembered that even if the way of humility and suffering love appears to fail, we are called to be faithful to the command and gifts of love which God has given to us. We should not be concerned with whether or not we ourselves will be hurt or ineffective. We should concentrate on being faithful to the way of love, to the example of Jesus. If we are faithful to the way of loving, humble nonviolence, it will appear as if we have failed. We may even appear to have failed as Jesus did when he was arrested and crucified. But we know that through our faithfulness and obedience to the gift of nonviolence which God has given us, God may use us and raise us to everlasting life as Jesus was raised up. If we continue to remember that we are one family, and to act in this reality by loving and overcoming evil, then God shall continue to live in our hearts and touch others and all of us to see with greater clarity the reality of God's reign.

The problem with the accusation that nonviolence does not work is that it reveals a failure to see that active nonviolence has already worked in the individual's heart, that it continually converts the individual person to a deeper reality, that it empowers the person with greater life and love, and that it enriches the person with dignity. The act of nonviolence converts our hearts from the state of the world to life in the kingdom of God.

When nonviolence has been used in history by large groups of people, it has often brought significant social change. The movements led by Gandhi and King accomplished sweeping reforms that changed history, without much bloodshed, compared to movements, wars and revolutions which use violence. Usually, when social change or revolution was called for in history, violence was used. We can say that violence (under the guise of a "means to an end," usually apparent victory and so-called "justice") never works because it only results in deaths and division, not the love and reconciliation which nonviolence seeks and captures. Nonviolence on public, massive levels has rarely been tried.

Many are confused by the whole concept of being willing to suffer in order to achieve more justice and peace. When we take the pain of violence on ourselves in order to restore justice, peace and truth, we are not approving the use of violence. We do not masochistically want to injure ourselves. We want our love to overcome the violence in ourselves and others, so that we may all be further reconciled and our lives and world redeemed. When such a step is made, it appears that we are allowing evil to happen.

Actually, we are uncovering the evil and violence that is already present in us, in our world, and we redeem it by not responding to it with further evil and violence but with love. Such active love which is willing to suffer for justice's sake will provoke people to unleash the violence in their hearts until they see that they are harming people just like themselves. The liberation campaigns of Gandhi and Martin Luther King, Jr. touched a nerve in their respective cultures causing people to persecute, arrest, and even kill the nonviolent campaigners. But the love of Gandhi and King and their co-workers overcame such evil and greater justice and reconciliation grew. The provocative love and truth of Jesus, it has been said, "caused people to do evil by crucifying him." Yet Jesus tried to show that any hate or alienation from the human family or from God's reign in one's heart is evil and violent. Jesus uncovered the violence we are willing to do to one another when we do not see one another as brothers and sisters, and he redeemed it, allowing us to see our mistakes, causing us to repent and love others as he did. The act of suffering in order to overcome evil and restore love is one of the most beautiful things a person can do with his or her life.

It has been charged that nonviolence shirks the responsibility of defending ourselves and others from evil. Instead, violence used against anyone goes against the responsibility God has given us to love one another. In our nonviolence, we take full responsibility for our own violence and the violence of others, and try to free ourselves and others from doing violence and to help all see that we are all equal. Violence used to defend ourselves and others does not redeem us or free us from violence or reconcile us. It only increases the vicious spiral of false peace, of further hate, violence and alienation. Our willingness to love others and to right wrongs by taking on suffering rather than inflicting it will cause others to see that their act of violence or hatred is not what they were created for, not what they really want to be about. It will free them and us to repent of the violence in our thoughts, words and deeds and to try to love. In this way, we take on our shoulders a much greater responsibility—the responsibility of reconciliation and love—and we can actually help others be good and do what is right and just. We take a great respect for all people, and do not judge them, but invite them through our love to a much fuller life. Creative nonviolent conflict resolutions have been used in history which were much more beneficial and reconciling for peoples on either side. Unfortunately, much human talent is spent on devising violent conflict resolutions when it could be spent in the act of service, nonviolent conflict resolution and reconciling love.

Some of these objections reveal a deeper problem. In many ways, we do not want real peace and reconciliation because it will be so costly. It will mean giving up many of our selfish ways and our possessions. We are too often afraid and insecure and thus prevented from acting. What we must do is act, in small steps, step by step, to promote love and truth by loving others, resisting evil, and taking on suffering. We must *try* nonviolence. This leap of faith and trust will free us from our fears and insecurities and then we can begin to take real responsibility.

The way of nonviolence asks much of a person; in fact, it demands one's whole life, sometimes one's very life. This high price is hard to pay and hard to accept. It is difficult to live out and often very painful, but, when done, extremely fulfilling and joyful. It is a gift of God and we need constantly to beg God for the grace of peace, for the desire to love others and to become more nonviolent and to be willing to suffer in order to right wrongs. Since God gives us the good gifts we ask for, often in better ways than we expected, we can be sure that this grace will be given if we pray hard and truly desire it with all our hearts and lives. It is impossible to live perfectly because we are sinful human beings and tend to forget who we are and what we are to do. But God loves each one of us very much and many people have come close to true nonviolence and have led lives very faithful to the will of God. All that is needed is the desire to live that life, the will to become nonviolent, the will to obey God, and perseverance and faithfulness. A vow of nonviolence is lived when one admits that one cannot be perfectly nonviolent in body and soul, surrenders to the power of God, lets go of all control, empties oneself and allows God to practice nonviolent love within oneself. In this way, the Spirit of nonviolence will live and work in us and love will live and flow in us. The loving, humble, nonviolent Christ will love others through that surrendered person and the grace of God will touch others. Nothing less than our whole lives are demanded in nonviolent love. Yet this high price is small in comparison to the gains of love, reconciliation and peace, the new friends made and community created, and the greater glory of God proclaimed.

8

Gandhi and the Vow of Nonviolence

Thomas Merton characterized the vows of nonviolence and truth which Gandhi professed as "the necessary preamble to the awakening of a mature political consciousness" and concluded that they "must be seen for what they are: not simply ascetic or devotional indulgences that may possibly suit the fancy of a few religious pacifists and confused poets, but precepts fundamentally necessary if humanity is to recover its right mind."[40] For Merton, Gandhi was "a model of integrity whom we cannot afford to ignore, and the one basic duty we all owe to the world of our time is to imitate him in 'disassociating ourselves from evil in total disregard of the consequences.' "[41]

What Merton realized was that the vow of nonviolence which Gandhi professed was indeed an able instrument of God's grace in the life of Gandhi, mediating enough moral strength for Gandhi to cling to his way of life religiously.

Gandhi became a world leader who demonstrated how nonviolence could be used and lived, personally and collectively. It is important to note that he saw the need in his life to profess vows in order for him to live according to the hard truths that he had learned through experimentation. The vow of nonviolence, which was first professed by Gandhi, was a great help to him, and his use of it should be considered as we begin a life pledged to nonviolence.

Mohandas Gandhi struggled throughout his life to be truthful and loving. He experimented, developed his ideas on nonviolence and love, and came to the conclusion that truth is God, the goal of life: "What I want to achieve— what I have been striving and pining to achieve these thirty years—is self-realization, to see God face to face. I live and move and have my being in pursuit of this goal."[42] Jim Douglass explains that Gandhi made God his end "not as a terminal point and his particular salvation but as the Reality to be progressively found through his daily politics, the ground and measure of every decision and as an end already visible in the faces of people resisting oppression with love."[43]

Gandhi's search for God led him in 1906 to choose to embrace celibacy. When he pledged a solemn vow to be celibate, he discovered the grace to live according to that way of life, "to live on the edge of a sword." "I realized that a vow, far from closing the door to real freedom," he wrote in this autobiography, "opened it. Up to this time I had not met with success because the will had been lacking, because I had had no faith in myself, no faith in the grace of God, and my mind had been tossed on the boisterous sea of doubt."[44] The vow proved to be an instrument of God's strength.

In September 1906, while Gandhi was in South Africa, a bill was passed that required all Indians to carry registration cards and violated other civil rights. He organized a mass meeting of Indians in Johannesburg to protest the bill. At that meeting, he urged Indians to vow themselves to resist injustice by using nonviolence. "The government has taken leave of all sense of decency," he said. "There is only one course open—to die rather than submit." The struggle for justice would be long and meant risking imprisonment, starvation, flogging and even death, he explained. "But I boldly declare, and with certainty, that so long as there is even a handful of men true to their pledge there can be only one end to the struggle—and that is victory." He asked everyone present to join him in a pledge of nonviolent resistance to any injustice and oppression, even unto death. The Indians stood, raised their hands, and vowed, "with God as our witness," not to submit to the ordinance if it became law.[45] Those pledges to be nonviolent and to resist injustice with one's life, by accepting suffering rather than inflicting it, made a deep impression on Gandhi. In those pledges, he found that people had the strength to stand up to overwhelming systemic evil and to remain human, to cling to their dignity, the truth of themselves as human beings. He realized that those vows unleashed a strong force of love and truth into society giving people the courage to do what was right in the face of great physical violence and even death. This lesson taught him that vows to do what is right, to be nonviolent, can be extremely helpful, motivating, and instrumental for a person who wants to be faithful to the highest ideals of truth and love.

Later, in 1919, many followers of Gandhi vowed themselves to nonviolence which committed them to resist the oppression and violence used by the British. On one occasion in Bombay, Gandhi commented on these vows of nonviolence: "Even such a mighty government as the Government of Britain must yield if we are true to our pledge. For the pledge is no small thing. It means a change of heart. It is an attempt to introduce the religious spirit into politics. We may no longer believe in the doctrine of 'tit for tat'; we may not meet hatred with hatred, violence with violence, evil with evil; but we have to make a continuous and persistent effort to return good for evil. . . . Nothing is impossible."[46] His vowed nonviolence aided him with the strength to suffer in his pursuit of justice, truth and love, rather than return violence with violence and hate.

Gandhi named his way of life, his pursuit of God, *satyagraha,* which means "holding on to truth," and, by extension, resistance to evil by the nonviolent means of voluntary suffering. The *satyagrahi,* for Gandhi, was the one who held steadfastly to God, dedicated his or her life to God, and was therefore a man or woman of God. The person who dedicated his or her self to this soul-force or truth-force needed to be disciplined in self-control, simplicity of life, suffering without fear or hatred, recognition of the unity of all living beings, and wholehearted service of others. In order to meet these disciplines and to remain faithful to the way of life dedicated to God, Gandhi professed many perpetual vows and encouraged the members of his Satyagraha Ashram at Sabarmati to profess them also. They pledged vows of truth, nonviolence, *brahmacharya* or celibacy, fearlessness, control of the palate, nonpossession, nonstealing, bread-labor, equality of religions, anti-untouchability, and *swadeshi* or using goods made locally or in one's own country.[47]

Gandhi later commented on such vows:

> Taking vows is not a sign of weakness, but of strength. To do at any cost something that one ought to do constitutes a vow. It becomes a bulwark of strength. A man who says that he will do something as far as possible betrays either his pride or his weakness. . . . God is the very image of the vow. God would cease to be God if he swerved from his own laws even by a hair's breadth. The sun is a greater keeper of observances; hence the possibility of measuring time and publishing almanacs. All business depends upon men fulfilling their promises. Are such promises less necessary in character

building or self-realization? We should therefore never
doubt the necessity of vows for the purpose of self-puri-
fication and self-realization.[48]

The vows were to be strictly followed as a means of pur-
suing God for all the members of Gandhi's ashram. He
found that he was able to live according to the truths he had
discovered because of his vows.

Gandhi's many experiments with truth in his own life
and in human situations released enormous energy, and his
commitment and faithfulness to his vows bore much fruit,
making possible many good things which had seemed to be
impossible to achieve. The vows were instruments that
kept him focused on God, on truth. He believed that everyone could discover and unleash the truths which he discovered simply by humbly experimenting in reality and by
applying the same dedication and faithfulness to the vows
of truth, nonviolence, celibacy, nonpossession, and the
other vows. "I have not the shadow of a doubt that any
man or woman can achieve what I have if he or she would
make the same effort and cultivate the same hope and
faith."[49]

His vow of nonviolence allowed him to remain humble, loving and steadfast in the face of extreme violence. He
was beaten up, thrown off a train, attacked and threatened
on many occasions, yet was always able to cling to a nonviolent attitude of openness, friendship, forgiveness and
love. His nonviolent witness and teachings inspired thousands of men and women to join him in campaigns of civil
disobedience. The history of his life is marked with periods
of fasting, years in prison, journal, newspaper and letter
writing, various campaigns for justice, such as the famous
salt march of 1930, and attempts to reconcile division
among people anywhere. His life was a prayerful attempt to

listen to the voice of God speaking to him, leading him, pointing him in the right direction in his efforts at peace-making. This cooperation with grace brought him great peace of heart and the justice and peace he sought in each campaign.

Gandhi realized that the faithful practice of his vows depended on God and this cooperation with God's grace through a life of prayer. Gandhi prayed daily to act out and remain faithful to his vows, saying:

> I will fear no one on earth today. I will fear only God.
> I will bear ill will to no one. I will accept injustice from
> no one. I will meet untruth with truth. In making truth
> known, I will accept all suffering.

Seven years before Gandhi was assassinated, he wrote, "I have been practicing with scientific precision nonviolence and its possibilities for an unbroken period of over fifty years. I have applied it in every walk of life—domestic, institutional, economic and political. I know of no single case in which it has failed. Where it has seemed sometimes to have failed, I have ascribed it to my imperfections. I claim no perfection for myself. But I do claim to be a passionate seeker after Truth, which is but another name for God. In the course of that search the discovery of nonviolence came to me. Its spread is my life mission. I have no interest in living except for the prosecution of that mission."[50]

Gandhi lived a committed life and remained faithful to the way of nonviolence through the harsh realities of the struggle for suffering love, by cooperating with the grace God gave to him to live and work in the world around him. "Nonviolence is not an easy thing to understand," he wrote, "still less to practice, weak as we are. We must all act prayerfully and humbly and continually ask God to open the eyes of our understanding, being ever ready to act according to the light as we daily receive it."[51]

Perhaps the best way to understand the depth of nonviolence which Gandhi approached can be seen at the moment of his death. In the summer of 1947, Gandhi proclaimed in a speech:

> Have I that nonviolence of the brave in me? My death alone will show that. If someone killed me and I died with prayer for the assassin on my lips, and God's remembrance and consciousness of His living presence in the sanctuary of my heart, then alone would I be said to have had the nonviolence of the brave.[52]

On January 29, 1948, the day before he was assassinated, Gandhi said to an associate:

> Note down this also, that if someone were to end my life by putting a bullet through me—as someone tried to do with a bomb the other day—and I met his bullet without a groan, and breathed my last taking God's name, then alone would I have made good my claim.[53]

This is precisely what happened. When Gandhi was shot, he was walking toward his evening prayer session and actually in the midst of making a greeting of peace and prayer toward his assailant. He died with God's name on his lips. This final act revealed that Gandhi was living out of a disarmed, peaceful heart that was united and rooted in prayer and love for all.

Gandhi was indeed deeply committed to the way of nonviolence. "My optimism rests on my belief in the infinite possibilities of the individual to develop nonviolence," he wrote. "The more you develop it in your own being, the more infectious it becomes till it overwhelms your surroundings and by and by might oversweep the world." He was convinced that "nonviolence is the greatest and most active force in the world. . . . One person who can express nonviolence in life exercises a force superior to all the forces of brutality."[54]

Gandhi wrote often about the strict attitude of humility this nonviolence must take: "I must reduce myself to zero. So long as a person does not of his or her own free will put himself or herself last among his or her fellow creatures, there is no salvation for him or her. Nonviolence is the farthest limit of humility."[55] He confessed: "I am but a poor struggling soul yearning to be wholly good—wholly truthful and wholly nonviolent in thought, word and deed, but ever failing to reach the ideal which I know to be true. It is a painful climb, but the pain of it is a positive pleasure to me. Each step upward makes me feel stronger and fit for the next."[56]

Gandhi characterized his life of vowed nonviolence as an effort to achieve an attitude of "desirelessness," that is, unattachment to anything but God the Truth. He understood vowed nonviolence as a life of "long training in self-denial and appreciation of the hidden forces within ourselves." He described a person approaching nonviolence and "desirelessness" as

> . . . a devotee who is jealous of none, who is a fount of mercy, who is without egotism, who is selfless, who treats alike cold and heat, happiness and misery, who is ever forgiving, who is always contented, whose resolutions are firm, who has dedicated mind and soul to God, who causes no dread, who is not afraid of others, who is free from exultation, sorrow and fear, who is pure, who is versed in action yet remains unaffected by it, who renounces all fruit, good or bad, who treats

friend and foe alike, who is untouched by respect or disrespect, who is not puffed up by praise, who does not go under when people speak ill of him, who loves silence and solitude, who has a disciplined reason.[57]

Nonviolence for Gandhi was a matter of the heart which affected one's relationship with others, and thus one's world. Thomas Merton saw that "for Gandhi, the spirit of nonviolence sprang from an inner realization of spiritual unity in himself." Merton wrote:

The whole Gandhian concept of nonviolent action and satyagraha is incomprehensible if it is to be thought as a means of achieving unity rather than as the fruit of inner unity already achieved. Indeed, this is the explanation for Gandhi's apparent failure (which became evident to him at the end of his own life). He saw that his followers had not reached the inner unity that he had realized in himself, and that their satyagraha was to a great extent a pretense since they believed it to be a means to achieve unity and freedom, while he saw that it must necessarily be the fruit of inner freedom. The thing of all and the most important of all was inner unity, the overcoming and healing of inner division, the consequent spiritual and personal freedom, of which autonomy and liberty were consequences.[58]

Merton recognized that nonviolence in Gandhi's life came from within, that from the love within Gandhi's heart and soul Gandhi was able to live and serve and love others. Merton also saw the connection between this life-result of a disarmed heart and the pledge Gandhi had originally made earlier to pursue and to commit himself to nonviolence.

There is indeed much to learn from Gandhi's prophetic life, from the vows he took, the commitments he fulfilled and the hoped for but sometimes unexpected results of reconciliation that did occur. We can take encouragement from Gandhi's lessons and experiments and the vow of nonviolence he professed, knowing that he remained committed to it and thought that others could, too. We can also take comfort in knowing that Gandhi did not know exactly what would happen once he risked the profession of his vow of nonviolence but that he deeply desired to be faithful and active to this way of God.

Besides learning from Gandhi's experiments in nonviolence and from his life, we who are considering the vow of nonviolence should turn to the life and example of Jesus of Nazareth, who is the model of nonviolence. Just as Gandhi was inspired to the way of nonviolence by the example of Jesus and especially the teachings of the Sermon on the Mount, so too should we look to the life and teachings of Jesus in order to find how to begin to move in the right direction for peace and love, to live out of a disarmed heart and to follow the nonviolent lead of God.

It is to Jesus of Nazareth, model of nonviolence, then, that we must turn finally in order to discover how to begin a life of committed nonviolence.

9

Jesus of Nazareth, Model of Nonviolence

We can just imagine the scene: a crowded synagogue on a sabbath day. Jesus is preaching as he often did. A man with a withered hand sits in the back among the crowd. Jesus notices him, and stops. He calls out to the man: "Stand up! Come out here in the middle." The man stands up and comes up front to the middle where he can be seen by everyone. Looking around the room, Jesus asks, "Is it against the law on the sabbath day to do good or to do evil? To save life or to kill?" There is no answer. Jesus looks around at them again. Finally, he says to the man, "Stretch out your hand." He stretches it out and his hand is better. The religious authorities are scandalized. They begin to discuss what they can do to destroy him.

Jesus had deliberately broken the rabbinical law. Jesus' act was public and provocative. He could not continue without stopping to heal the withered hand of a person. He did so knowing that by this act he would get himself into trouble. Jesus is nonviolent and active, resisting death and choosing life. It is for this reason, this story and the many other stories like it, that Jesus is the model of nonviolence. He always provokes and urges people to do good; he always says no to death, chooses life, and loves others in the truth.

Jesus was born into the world of the poor, in a humble, simple situation, into a poor family. Throughout his life, he embraced a way of love and truth. He taught and lived non-violence and showed that anyone can be nonviolent by becoming poor, humbling oneself and faithfully accepting God's spirit of nonviolence. In his very active life, his resistance to evil, his forgiveness and compassion, his active love for others, Jesus revealed that God is nonviolent, always acting in a manner of love and truth. In fact, Jesus revealed that love and truth are God, that God is present in the Spirit of love and truth.

After fasting for forty days in the desert, Jesus returned to Galilee proclaiming with great optimism that the reign of God is here and now. He taught his followers to live in this freedom. His message was: "The reign of God is at hand. Repent, believe the good news, be nonviolent, love and forgive one another." At the center of his message was the command to love God by loving one's neighbor, that is, to practice *agape,* the foundation of the Sermon on the Mount and all the teachings and parables of Jesus. In the story of the Good Samaritan (Lk 10:25–37), Jesus explained that one's neighbor was any human being in any kind of immediate need and that love was manifested in immediate action toward that person directed to meet that need. Jesus taught that this was a way in which we could love God.

Jesus' command of love demanded the unprecedented requirement of loving one's enemies:

> I say this to you who are listening: Love your enemies, do good to those who hate you, bless those who curse you, pray for those who treat you badly. To the person who slaps you on one cheek, present the other cheek too; to the person who takes your cloak from you, do not refuse your tunic. Give to everyone who asks you, and do not ask for your property back from the person

who robs you. Treat others as you would like them to treat you. If you love those who love you, what thanks can you expect? Even sinners love those who love them. And if you do good to those who do good to you, what thanks can you expect? For even sinners do that much. And if you lend to those from whom you hope to receive, what thanks can you expect? Even sinners lend to sinners to get back the same amount. Instead, love your enemies and do good, and lend without any hope of return. You will have a great reward, and you will be sons and daughters of the Most High, for he himself is kind to the ungrateful and the wicked. Be compassionate as your Father is compassionate (Lk 6:27–36).

Jesus invited people to a life of militant resistance to evil by loving every human being including persecutors and enemies. In the Sermon on the Mount, Jesus taught that the reign of God belongs first and foremost to the poor, to the powerless, to those persecuted for the sake of justice. Jesus insisted that we must always seek reconciliation before everything else we do, even before going to a communal worship service. Not only are we not to kill, he said, but we are not even to be angry with one another. He encouraged his friends not to cooperate with violence by returning violence with violence:

Offer the wicked person no resistance. On the contrary, if anyone hits you on the right cheek, offer him the other as well; if a man takes you to law and would have your tunic, let him have your cloak as well. And if anyone orders you to go one mile, go two miles with him. Give to anyone who asks, and if anyone wants to borrow, do not turn away (Mt 5:38–42).

Jesus' way of love did not mean passivity or apathy but meant standing up for what was right. It meant noncooperation with evil and violence and overcoming that evil and violence through love and truth and a willingness to suffer for love and truth.

The attitude of nonresistance and nonretaliation to violence which Jesus commended is fully intertwined with his command of active love, the love of enemies. These active commands of love are rooted in the "very nature of God," as Ron Sider explains: "Instead of promptly destroying sinners, God continues lovingly to shower the good gifts of creation upon them. Since that is the way God is, those who want to be God's sons and daughters must do likewise."[59]

Jesus commended many practical suggestions on how to live and find life in the kingdom of God in the present moment. He recommended giving, praying, fasting, trusting, and setting our hearts on God's kingdom and God's righteousness first. Jesus called for total simplicity and a radical dependence on God, for his followers to live as children. He said, "Do not worry. Do not be afraid. Do not judge." Jesus was not afraid, and he said we do not have to be afraid either. He taught us not to fear the power of violence, the power of death, the powers that can kill. He showed a way out of our fears. He called for a real trust in God which would not allow the use of violence and retaliation to violence. He commended perseverance and promised we would be persecuted if we tried to become nonviolent, to resist evil and to choose life.

In the portrait of the last judgment (Mt 25:31–46), Jesus taught that God dwells in every human being and that all people are equal, that whatever one does to another human being, one does to a sister or brother and to God. In this story, Jesus says God commends those who have treated others with respect, dignity, kindness, forgiveness and love. God will say to the humble:

> Take for your heritage the kingdom prepared for you since the foundation of the world. For I was hungry and you gave me food; I was thirsty and you gave me drink; I was a stranger and you made me welcome; naked and you clothed me; sick and you visited me; in prison and you came to see me. . . . I tell you solemnly, in so far as you did this to one of the least of these brothers or sisters of mine, you did it to me. . . . In so far as you neglected to do this to one of the least of these, you neglected to do it to me.

With this story, Jesus urges us to remember who we are, that we are all one family, all equal, and to act in that memory, to treat one another as brothers and sisters.

Jesus' provocative love is recounted over and over again in the many stories of the Gospel, from the time his disciples picked corn illegally on the sabbath, to eating regularly with marginalized peoples such as tax collectors, to healing people in public places and challenging the laws. Jesus taught people to love one another, saying, "A person can have no greater love than to lay down his life for his friends." By going to Jerusalem and the cross, by risking the possibility of an early death, Jesus demonstrated his great love for all people and the nonviolence in his heart. He showed through his actions—and the ultimate action of laying down his life for others—how we can love one another: by living in the truth all our days, by forgiving in the face of death, and by challenging the powers of death and violence at the same time.

Jesus was brought before the government leader in Jerusalem and was charged: "We found this man inciting our people to revolt, opposing payment of the tribute to

Caesar, proclaiming to be Christ, a king" (Lk 23:2). His accusers persisted: "He is inflaming the people with his teaching all over Judea. It has come all the way from Galilee where he started down to here." His teachings and acts of love and truth had made him a threat to the religious and civil authorities because people were beginning to treat one another in a new and drastic way—to believe that they could love one another to the point of sharing all their possessions, property, food, talents and their very lives with each other. Where there was oppression or violence, he exposed the truth, by being truthful. When the Pharisees had tried to trap him earlier, one of them began by saying: "Master, we know that you are an honest man and teach the way of God in an honest way and that you are not afraid of anyone because a person's rank means nothing to you" (Mt 22:16).

The decision to go to Jerusalem marked the depth of his commitment to nonviolence because he knew, as his disciples knew, of the opposition that awaited him there and that speaking openly would endanger his life. And yet, he went to call the religious and civil authorities, and all the people of Jerusalem, back to their identities as God's children. He went to preach and act in a manner of nonviolence in disregard of the consequences. His decision to go to Jerusalem was an act of trust in God in the midst of a dangerous situation. Jesus was not passive; he went and provoked trouble by exposing and revealing truth and calling for conversion of heart. Jesus had taught nonviolence and love of enemies, so it was fitting for him to put aside fears and to invite others to put aside their fears and be children of God. He could have remained in Galilee and continued his "successful" ministry of preaching, enjoying the respect and adulation of those who sought him out. His

friends had told him not to go because it was too dangerous. But he decided to go to Jerusalem.

The passion narratives of the four Gospels form an
account of a man who urgently wanted peace for his people
and who was deeply aware of how the world had avoided
and misunderstood so much about love and truth. In Jerusalem, he proclaimed his vision in a spirit of nonviolence
by calling for truth everywhere. His moral power challenged the chief priests and scribes, and he even took nonviolent direct action by trying to open the temple to all. His
cleansing of the temple was a small, direct, public act which
called for integrity and real faith and which was intended
to help us to remember who we are and to reconcile us.
This insistence left him open to attack, yet he was willing
to face the consequences for righting what he saw as wrong.

The night before he died, when he knew full well that
action would soon be taken against him, he brought his
friends together and encouraged them to form a community of peace and love, to live together as God's children,
to share a meal together and to remember him and his way
of nonviolence by doing so. He instructed his friends to
serve one another as he continued to do that night by sym-
bolically and actually bending over and washing their dirty
feet.

The authorities realized that they would lose their
power if enough people believed and acted out what Jesus
taught—that people should obey God and love one another
and not support governments through blind obedience and
violence against one another. In the garden of Gethsemane,
he showed his perseverance by continuing on the way of
nonviolence. "Father, let your will be done, not mine," he
prayed. When the soldiers arrived asking for Jesus, he said,
"I have told you I am he. . . . If I am the one you want, let
these others go" (Jn 18:8). He was taken away as a criminal.

Jesus was faithful to the way of nonviolence and did not return the insults and violence used against him with his own violence because he knew these people as his brothers and sisters. He resisted nonviolently by speaking with truth and love and by forgiving them. When questioned by the high priest, Jesus answered: "I have spoken openly for all the world to hear. I have always taught in the synagogue and in the temple, where all the Jews meet together. I have said nothing in secret. . . . Ask my hearers what I taught; they know what I said." After saying this, one of the guards slapped Jesus in the face and asked, "Is that the way to answer the high priest?"

Jesus spoke up. He did not strike back, but insisted on truth, saying: "If there is something in what I said, point it out. But if there is no offense in it, why do you strike me?" (Jn 18:23).

When he was condemned by the high priest, Jesus was punched, spat on, blindfolded, hit in the face with fists and mocked. Jesus experienced the pain of nonviolent suffering love and suffered the blows, the hurt, and the abuse without striking back, condemning or denying the truth about his message and his identity as Child of God. In his agony, he still did not resort to the same violence used against him, and this profound nonviolence reveals the divinity of his spirit of love and truth. Before Pilate, he said, "Mine is not a kingdom of this world. If my kingdom were of this kind, my people would have fought to prevent my being surrendered to the Jews. But my kingdom is not of this kind. . . . I was born for this. I came into the world for this: to bear witness to the truth. All who are on the side of truth listen to my voice" (Jn 18:35–37). In the reign in which Jesus lives, violence is not used, allowed or accepted. In the world, violence is the force that is respected and honored and used to destroy truthful people like Jesus of Nazareth.

Jesus was betrayed and denied by close friends, scourged, crowned with twisted thorns, and dressed in a purple robe. After carrying the cross, he was stripped and nailed naked to the cross, suffering great physical pain and verbal abuse. In the agony of crucifixion, Jesus responded with pure nonviolence, continuing to see his persecutors as children of God. Instead of hating those who were executing him, he took the most courageous step possible: he forgave his executioners and those who had hurt him. He prayed for them: "Father, forgive them. They do not know what they are doing." He recognized that they had forgotten who they were and who they were called to be, and so he did not pass judgment on them nor did he condemn them. He forgave them and continued to love them. His forgiving act revealed his great love, his faithfulness and obedience to God, and the living reality of the kingdom of God in his heart. Hanging naked on the cross, Jesus was completely disarmed and responded only with love, forgiveness and truth. He was jeered at by passers-by as he was dying, and yet he remained faithful to who he was and to what God wanted him to do. He and his message were misunderstood and mocked. By trusting in God, Jesus performed the truly humble act of nonviolence, trusting when there seemed to be no hope. His final words conveyed the life commitment of his love for God: "Father, into your hands I commend my spirit." To the end, Jesus remained faithful to the truth of his vision of the reign of God. Jesus, the model of nonviolence, loved all men and women at great pain and cost to himself. His death on the cross was a direct result of his total love for all people and his commitment to the truth. His death on the cross was the final stage of his continuing humble plea for life, love and truth. By entering into an unjust, brutal death with humility and powerlessness, Jesus revealed the way of redemptive suffering love. The crucifixion and death of Jesus was a complete scandal and failure in the eyes of his family, friends, and country men and women. The cross was the sign of utter disapproval and rejection, and in it Jesus accepted misunderstanding and failure. He nonetheless hoped in God in the midst of this rejection. In death, Jesus clung to the reality of the reign of God in all its fullness of truth and love. In giving up his life for others and bringing life to others, Jesus lived every moment of his life knowing God reigns, living in the kingdom of God until his last breath and helping others to see that. The crucified, disarmed loving Jesus is the perfect image of God who is nonviolent, a God who calls people to life even as they kill him. It is this nonviolent Jesus who invites others to follow him in the way of humble nonviolence.

The words spoken to the women who came to the tomb of Jesus that following Sunday morning are words that have changed the darkness of pain into glorious light: "There is no reason to be afraid. I know you are looking for Jesus who was crucified. He is not here, for he has risen." These are words of great joy and wonder. The revelation of the resurrection of Jesus is the ultimate affirmation of the way of nonviolence by God. The resurrection of Jesus proclaims that Jesus' vision of the unity of the human family is correct and that he was right to act in a spirit of nonviolence, forgiving love and humble truth. God raised Jesus and through his resurrection invited all people to live as Jesus did. The resurrection of Jesus is proof that his message and humble life of nonviolence are the right way to live. The risen Jesus Christ transformed his disciples and changed their lives; they understood then and fully accepted the reign of God, the way of nonviolence. The disciples realized that God had affirmed Jesus' life of nonviolence. No longer did they misunderstand the folly of the cross, the scandalous love which is nonviolence. The disciples thereafter accepted that nonviolent suffering love is the way of God, that God is indeed reigning, that the love of God is stronger than violence or death itself, and that if one places all trust in God and follows the way of love and nonviolence, everlasting life and love will reign in their hearts. They were able to see the real effect of committed nonviolence and the reality of Jesus' promise: "Take courage. I have conquered the world." Jesus, the fullness of humble nonviolence, did indeed conquer the world of violence and death; his spirit and way of life have continued to move people beyond the world of violence into the reign of love and peace for almost two thousand years.

The first gift the risen Jesus Christ gave to his disciples was the Spirit of nonviolence. "Peace be with you," he said. It is only in the light of this resurrection, the fullest demonstration of the nonviolent power of God's reign, that Jesus' gift of peace, "a peace which the world cannot give," can be understood.[60] After his resurrection, Jesus fully explained his life of nonviolent love, his willingness to suffer and the glorious revelation of affirmation which was the resurrection:

"This is what I meant when I said, while I was still with you, that everything written about me in the law of Moses, in the Prophets and in the Psalms, had to be fulfilled." He then opened their minds to understand the scriptures, and he said to them, "So you see how it is written that the Christ would suffer and on the third day rise from the dead, and that, in his name, repentance for the forgiveness of sins would be preached to all the nations, beginning from Jerusalem. You are witnesses to this. And now I am sending down to you what the Father has promised. Stay in the city then, until you

are clothed with the power from on high" (Lk 24:44–
49).

The resurrection of Jesus helped his disciples to understand
nonviolence. They were transformed and began lives committed to him and his nonviolence. He missioned them to
teach everyone about his life of nonviolent suffering love
and the good news that everyone can live this new way of
life. He sent his disciples to invite others to follow his
example. They were sent to become ministers of reconciliation who would reunite the human family, work to end
violence, and create a community of love and peace. They
were to continue forming humanity into a nonviolent
community.

The risen Lord said to his friends: "Go, make disciples
of all nations. Baptize them . . . and teach them to observe
all the commands I gave you. And know that I am with you
always; yes, to the end of time." In this final command,
Jesus was reiterating what he had said in the Sermon on the
Mount: "Your light must shine before men and women so
that they may see goodness in your acts and give praise to
God" (Mt 5:16).

> Anyone who desires to come to me will hear my words
> and put them into practice. I will show you with whom
> that person is to be compared. He or she may be lik-
> ened to the man who, in building a house, dug deeply
> and laid the foundation on a rock. When the floods
> came the torrent rushed in on that house, but failed to
> shake it because of its solid foundation. On the other
> hand, anyone who has heard my words but not put
> them into practice is like the man who built his house
> on the ground without any foundation. When the tor-
> rent rushed upon it, it immediately fell in and was
> completely destroyed (Mt 6:47–49).

Jesus taught them that if they want to live as he lived, to follow him, they cannot simply hear the word of nonviolence. They must act on it. This teaching remains his final mission to his disciples—in effect: "Go and act nonviolently. Love one another. Put into practice what I have taught you and help others to observe these commands also."

The vow of nonviolence is the acceptance of Jesus' mission to love others and to hold on to the truth, to follow Jesus wholeheartedly by learning about nonviolence and putting it into practice in one's life. The vow of nonviolence is an instrument intended to help the follower of Jesus live faithfully this life of active nonviolence. In light of Jesus' outspoken stance against the state, his own murder and subsequent resurrection, those vowed to nonviolence will fast, pray, study, dialogue, act nonviolently, serve the poor, go to prison in the nonviolent struggle for love, be crucified and rise again. They will do as Jesus did: act in a spirit of love and truth in all the wrong places at the wrong times to the wrong people and accept the consequences for such love: crucifixion and resurrection, pain and joy, isolation and community, death and everlasting life.

Conclusion

Lanza del Vasto went to India from his home in France in the 1930's on a spiritual pilgrimage. After a long time of searching and listening, he decided to return to France to teach people about nonviolence and to practice it among his country men and women. One evening before going back, he told his story over a period of hours to Gandhi. "He listened to me with great patience," Lanza del Vasto recalled later. Then Gandhi said to him:

> Yes, it would be good if you teach them; you are one of theirs after all. And if you teach them nonviolence, they will listen. I know that I can't, because even if they accept the idea they couldn't handle it. Yes, and it would be beautiful. But what I want to know is, are you called? Because if you are not, you may be full of courage, ready to sacrifice, intelligent, and yet nothing will come of it. And if you are called, everything shall be given to you, the means and the knowledge and strength that you need for the accomplishment of your mission.[61]

In the search for truth, we must listen to the voice of God, calling us, leading us. As we practice active nonviolence, experiment in truth and listen to God, God will speak to us and invite us to follow the Spirit of love and truth down a particular path. We can be at great peace

120

knowing that God is with us—encouraging us, leading us, calling us—and knowing that we are not alone.

In committing ourselves to nonviolence, we must act, reflect, study and share with one another, but always listen to God and hear in what direction we are being called. As we cooperate with God's grace, we can let go of all control, be at peace, know that God is forming us into instrument's of God's peace, and know that somehow our lives will bear fruit.

After being moved to vow nonviolence, I was led, among other places, to Central America for a short while, where daily bombings, fear, war and death were all around me. In confronting the realities of violence and fear, I tried to remember that we are all brothers and sisters and to love all those I encountered, including those who held machine guns and questioned me for my solidarity with the poor. Entering into the powerlessness of the suffering and oppressed peoples gave me renewed inner peace and a spirit of forgiveness and love that encouraged me to try to love enemies. I would say that the vow of nonviolence which I professed opened up a channel of grace for me, empowering me to choose life and to resist death. This does not mean that I am holy or nonviolent. I am a sinner, a violent person, trying to become nonviolent and to love others. The vow of nonviolence, as a channel of grace, opened my heart to desire further to follow the way of nonviolence and to continue the commitment of searching that is involved, even in the midst of violence and war into which I was brought.

The vow of nonviolence, in conclusion, is the sign of a choice made in one's heart to accept the nonviolence which God has offered and to follow the call of God along God's way of nonviolence. We want to become nonviolent because Jesus is nonviolent, because God is nonviolent and calls us to become nonviolent people.

Gandhi wrote that "the business of every God-fearing person is to disassociate himself or herself from evil—in total disregard of the consequences. He or she must have faith in a good deed producing only a good result. . . . He or she follows the truth though the following of it may endanger his or her very life. He or she knows that it is better to die in the way of God than to live in the way of Satan."[62] The choice for us between the two ways remains: we can choose the way of Christ, the way of nonviolence, or the way of fear and violence. The daily choice for Christ and his way of nonviolence will mean taking greater risks with our lives and being more creative with our nonviolence in order to be faithful to the level of trust, dependence and grace which we have been called to.

What is needed today is a renewal of nonviolence in every facet of life. For Christians to become better followers of Jesus, we need to become better practitioners of nonviolence. Christians and all people are being invited in this day and age to a deeper level and practice of nonviolence: in our communities, in our families, with our friends, in our public witness and in our willingness to risk our lives for those who are suffering.

The nonviolent Spirit that God offers to us will continually empower us to believe that each one of us can do something for those who are suffering, that our actions of nonviolence, no matter how small or how public or how apparently ineffective, will help us to love one another better and reconcile us. Not only must Christians be willing to spend their lives in the service of the oppressed through nonviolence, but a spiritual revolution must occur, a deepening of the level of nonviolence in our lives and in our relationships with others. A whole new way of thinking is being called for, a totally integrated nonviolent attitude. We must put on the mind of Christ, and reflect his nonviolence so that "the will and the work of God may be done" in us (Phil 2:14).

Thomas Merton concluded that the duty of the Christian in our day and age is to work "for the total abolition of war." He wrote in *The Catholic Worker* in 1964 that the Church must "lead the way on the road to nonviolent settlement of difficulties and toward the gradual abolition of war as the way of settling international or civil disputes. Christians must become active in every possible way.... Prayer and sacrifice must be used as the most effective spiritual weapons in the war against war, and like all weapons, they must be used with deliberate aim: not just with a vague aspiration for peace and security, but against violence and war. This implies that we are also willing to sacrifice and restrain our own instinct for violence and aggressiveness in our relations with other people.... This is the great Christian task of our time." Just before Merton was accidentally killed in Bangkok, he told another participant at the interfaith conference he was attending: "What we are asked to do at present is not so much to speak of Christ as to let him live in us so that people may find him by feeling how he lives in us."[63]

We can allow Christ to live in us by allowing the nonviolence of Christ to become part of our very being. The nonviolence of the vowed life permeates every facet of our lives, reigns in every encounter with another person and in every public witness to the love of God.

The vow of nonviolence is a pledge to accept and live out the gift of nonviolence which God has so graciously given. The vow of nonviolence is a recognition of who we are—people disarmed by God who want to be faithful and to continue to choose God's nonviolence and loving disarmament. It is a good thing for now, an instrument for calling our Christian communities back to their roots of lived nonviolence. When it becomes explicit that being a Christian is being nonviolent, the vow as such may no longer be necessary because what is implicit will be explicit. We are called to nonviolence; the vow of nonviolence is a pledge to witness to all people about God's love and truth, and a pledge to begin and to continue the journey of Christian nonviolence to God.

Christians can begin the road of living out nonviolence in their actions and continue to cultivate it in their hearts. We must try to be nonviolent to ourselves, to others, to God. In the process, we must allow God to enter into us and overcome our fears to the point where we embrace death and everlasting life without fear and enter into that Reality that we have known all along. We hope, then, to be united with everyone in the light of God, where we are one family, and where we will never forget that.

This book is just a small invitation to a way of being faithful to our identity and mission founded in God's nonviolence. We are called to witness. We want our witness to be an instrument of God's conversion of the world of violence into a world of nonviolence, a world of love and truth. Let us witness, then, and be faithful to the way of life God is calling us and leading us to live. Let us allow God's love and truth to disarm our hearts and let us witness to this loving action of God, so that the Spirit of Love and Truth will move in us and our brothers and sisters more and more, disarming hearts and disarming nations.

Notes

1. Charles McCarthy, *Christian Nonviolence: Option or Obligation?* (Unpublished, transcript of video series, available from AGAPE, 918 North Main Street, Brockton, Mass. 02401), page "6-1."

2. McCarthy, p. "8-5."

3. Stephen B. Oates, *Let the Trumpet Sound: The Life of Martin Luther King, Jr.* (NY: New American Library Inc., 1982), pp. 89–90.

4. McCarthy, p. "10-4."

5. Martin Luther King, Jr., *Stride Toward Freedom* (New York: Harper and Row, 1958), p. 84.

6. King, pp. 87–88.

7. Gerard Vanderhaar, *Nonviolence: Theory and Practice* (Pax Christi, USA, 1980), p. 6.

8. *The Code of Canon Law* (Grand Rapids: Eerdmans, 1983), p. 210.

9. McCarthy, *ibid.,* pp. "1-11."

10. Joseph Fahey, "Peace, War and the Christian Conscience" (Christopher Publications, 1982), p. 10.

11. Gerard Vanderhaar, *Christians and Nonviolence in the Nuclear Age* (Mystic, CT: Twenty-Third Publ., 1982), pp. 16–18. Further references to Vanderhaar are to this book.

12. *Ibid.,* p. 22; Jim Wallis (ed.), *Waging Peace* (San Francisco: Harper and Row, 1981), p. 2.

13. Vanderhaar, p. 25.

14. "To Be or Not To Be" (Christopher Publications, 1981); *Newsweek,* December 5, 1983, p. 56.

15. Vanderhaar, p. 28.

16. These facts are taken from: W. Brandt, *North-South,* MIT Press, 1980; United Nations Press Release; Disarmament Fact Sheet, Public Relations, UN Document A/35/392; East African Fact Sheet: Am. Friends Service Committee; Presidential Commission Report on World Hunger, 1981.

17. Presidential Commission Report on World Hunger, 1981.

18. Edward Rice, *The Man in the Sycamore Tree* (NY: Doubleday, 1970), p. 89.

19. Martin Luther King, Jr. *Why We Can't Wait* (NY: Mentor Books, 1963), pp. 63–64.

20. John Howard Yoder, "Living the Disarmed Life," in *Waging Peace,* Jim Wallis (ed.), p. 132.

21. James Douglass, *Lightning East to West* (NY: Crossroad, 1983), p. 7.

22. Francis Britto, S.J., "On the Relevance of Gandhian Nonviolence" (unpublished, 1984).

23. Thomas Merton, *Gandhi on Nonviolence* (NY: New Directions, 1984), p. 29.

24. "Nonviolent Direct Action," IFOR Report Supplement, December 1983.

25. Britto, *ibid.*

26. John Kavanaugh, S.J., *Following Christ in a Consumer Society* (Maryknoll: Orbis Books, 1981), pp. 121–122.

27. James Douglass, *The Non-Violent Cross: A Theology of Revolution and Peace* (NY: Macmillan, 1968), p. 35.

28. Mohandas Gandhi, *An Autobiography* (Boston: Beacon Press, 1957), p. 6.

29. Gerard Vanderhaar, *ibid.,* p. 107.

30. Henri J. M. Nouwen, "The Monk and the Cripple: Toward a Spirituality of Ministry," *America,* March 15, 1980, pp. 205–210.

31. Joyce Hollyday, "Bathed in the Spirit: The Story of Peace Pentecost," *Sojourners,* Vol. 12, no. 7, August 1983, pp. 24–31.

32. George Aschenbrenner, S.J., "Comparison and Competition: Stifling Spiritual Intimacy," *Review for Religious,* Vol. 38, no. 6, 1979, pp. 924–931.

33. Jim Wallis, *Revive Us Again: A Sojourner's Story* (Nashville: Abingdon Press, 1983), pp. 155–156.

34. Gandhi, *ibid.*

35. Vanderhaar, *ibid.,* pp. 105–106.

36. Roland Bainton, *Christian Attitudes Toward War and Peace* (NY: Abingdon Press, 1960), pp. 66–84.

37. C. John Cadoux, *The Early Christian Attitude to War* (NY: Seabury, 1982), p. 245.

38. Bainton, *ibid.;* Mary Lou Kownacki, "A Vow of Nonviolence," *Christian Witness,* Erie, Pa., Winter 1985.

39. Jim Wallis, *Agenda for Biblical People* (San Francisco: Harper and Row, 1984), pp. 22, 73, 74.

40. Thomas Merton, *The Nonviolent Alternative* (NY: Farrar, Straus, Giroux, 1971, 1980), pp. 178–184; Merton, *Gandhi on Nonviolence,* p. 20.

41. Merton, *The Nonviolent Alternative* (NY: Farrar, Straus, Giroux, 1971, 1980), pp. 178–184.

42. Gandhi, *An Autobiography,* p. 6.

43. James Douglass, *The Non-Violent Cross,* p. 34.

44. Gandhi, *An Autobiography,* pp. 180–181.

45. Calvin Kytle, *Gandhi, Soldier of Nonviolence* (Washington, D.C: Seven Locks Press, 1982), pp. 90–91; Louis Fischer, *The Life of Mahatma Gandhi* (NY: Harper and Row, 1950), pp. 75–76.

46. Fischer, p. 177.

47. Mohandas Gandhi, *Nonviolent Resistance* (NY: Schocken Books, 1951), p. iii.

48. *Ibid.,* p. 37–38.

49. Philip Berrigan, *Widen the Prison Gates* (NY: Simon and Schuster, 1973), pp. 174–175.

50. Gandhi, *All Men Are Brothers* (NY: Continuum, 1982), p. 87.

51. *Ibid.,* p. 89.

52. *Ibid.,* p. 49.

53. *Ibid.,* p. 50.

54. Merton, *Gandhi on Nonviolence,* p. 25.

55. Douglass, *Lightning East to West,* pp. 17–40.

56. Gandhi, *All Men Are Brothers,* p. 54.

57. Louis Fischer, *Gandhi: His Life and Message for the World* (NY: Mentor Books, 1954), p. 18.

58. Merton, *Gandhi on Nonviolence,* p. 6.

59. Ron Sider, "Reconciling Our Enemies," in Jim Wallis (ed.), *Waging Peace,* p. 141.

60. "The Challenge of Peace: God's Challenge and Our Response." A pastoral letter by the U.S. Catholic Conference of Bishops, 1983, 39–55.

61. Lanza Del Vasto, "Nonviolence: A Lesson in Arithmetic," *The Catholic Worker,* Jan. 1977, p. 3.

62. Thomas Merton, *Conjectures of a Guilty Bystander* (NY: Doubleday and Co., 1966), p. 102.

63. James Forest, *Thomas Merton* (NY: Paulist Press, 1980), pp. 73–79, 99.

Suggested Readings

Bainton, Roland. *Christian Attitudes Toward War and Peace.* New York: Abingdon, 1960.

Berrigan, Daniel, *Ten Commandments for the Long Haul.* Nashville: Abingdon, 1981.

Berrigan, Philip. *Widen the Prison Gates.* New York: Simon and Schuster, 1973.

Bondurant, Joan. *Conquest of Violence: The Gandhian Philosophy of Conflict.* Berkeley: Univ. of Cal. Press, 1969.

Bonhoeffer, Dietrich. *The Cost of Discipleship.* New York: Macmillan, Co., 1937, 1977.

Cadoux, C. John. *The Early Christian Attitude to War.* New York: Seabury, 1982.

Day, Dorothy. *The Long Loneliness.* New York: Harper and Row, 1981.

————. *Loaves and Fishes.* San Francisco: Harper and Row, 1983.

Door, Donald. *Option for the Poor.* Maryknoll: Orbis, 1983.

Douglass, James. *Lightning East to West.* New York: Crossroad, 1983.

————. *The Non-Violent Cross: A Theology of Revolution and Peace.* New York: Macmillan, 1968.

————. *Resistance and Contemplation.* New York: Doubleday, 1971.

Erikson, Erik. *Gandhi's Truth.* New York: Norton, 1969.

Fischer, Louis. *The Life of Mahatma Gandhi.* New York: Harper and Row, 1950, 1983.

Fuller, R. and I., eds. *Essays on the Love Commandment.* Philadelphia, Fortress, 1978.

Gandhi, Mohandas. *All Men Are Brothers.* New York: Continuum, 1982.

—————. *An Autobiography or The Story of My Experiments in Truth.* Boston: Beacon, 1957.

—————. *Nonviolent Resistance.* New York: Schocken Books 1951.

Grannis, Christopher; Laffin, Arthur; Schade, Elin. *The Risk of the Cross.* New York: Seabury, 1981.

Gregg, Richard. *The Power of Nonviolence.* New York: Schocken, 1966.

Gutierrez, Gustavo. *The Power of the Poor in History.* Maryknoll: Orbis, 1983.

Häring, Bernard. *Dare To Be Christian.* Liguori, Miss.: Liguori, 1983.

Hauerwas, Stanley. *The Peaceable Kingdom: A Primer in Christian Ethics.* Univ. of Notre Dame Press, 1983.

Hellwig, Monika. *Jesus: The Compassion of God.* Wilmington: Michael Glazier, 1984.

—————. *The Eucharist and the Hunger of the World.* New York: Paulist, 1976.

Kavanaugh, John Francis, S.J. *Following Christ in a Consumer Society: The Spirituality of Cultural Resistance.* Maryknoll: Orbis, 1982.

King, Jr. Martin Luther, *Strength To Love.* Philadelphia: Fortress, 1963, 1981.

—————. *Stride Toward Freedom.* New York: Harper and Row, 1958.

—————. *Where Do We Go From Here?* New York: Harper and Row, 1967.

—————. *Why We Can't Wait.* New York: Mentor, 1963.

Kytle, Calvin. *Gandhi, Soldier of Nonviolence.* Washington, D.C: Seven Locks, 1982.

Macgregor, G. H. C. *The New Testament Basis of Pacifism.* New York: Fellowship, 1941, 1971.

Matura, Thaddee. *Gospel Radicalism.* Maryknoll: Orbis, 1984.

McKenzie, John. *The Power and the Wisdom.* New York: Bruce, 1965.

McSorley, Richard, S.J. *New Testament Basis of Peacemaking.* Scottdale, Pa.: Herald, 1985.

Merton, Thomas. *Conjectures of a Guilty Bystander.* New York: Doubleday, 1966.

————— (ed.). *Gandhi on Nonviolence.* New York: New Directions, 1964.

—————. *New Seeds of Contemplation.* New York: New Directions, 1961.

—————. *The Nonviolent Alternative.* New York: Farrar, Straus, Giroux, 1971, 1980.

Miller, William D. *Dorothy Day: A Biography.* New York: Harper and Row, Pub., 1982.

Miller, William Robert. *Nonviolence.* New York: Schocken, 1964.

Oates, Stephen. *Let the Trumpet Sound: The Life of Martin Luther King, Jr.* New York: Plume, 1982.

Quigley, Margaret and Garvey, Michael. *The Dorothy Day Book.* Springfield, Ill.: Templegate Pub., 1982.

Rice, Edward. *The Man in the Sycamore Tree.* New York: Doubleday, 1970.

Schell, Jonathan. *The Fate of the Earth.* New York: Knopf, 1981.

Sharp, Gene. *Gandhi as a Political Strategist.* Boston: Porter Sargent, 1979.

—————. *The Politics of Nonviolent Action* (3 vols.). Boston: Porter Sargent, 1973.

Sider, Ron. *Christ and Violence.* Scottdale, Pa.: Herald, 1979.

Sider, Ron and Taylor, Richard. *Nuclear Holocaust and Christian Hope.* Downers Grove, Ill.: InterVarsity, 1982.

Thoreau, Henry David. *Walden* and *On the Duty of Civil Disobedience.* New York: New American Library, 1960.

Tolstoy's Writings on Nonviolence and Civil Disobedience. New York: Bergman, 1967.

Trocme, Andre. *Jesus and the Nonviolent Revolution.* Scottdale, Pa.: Herald, 1973.

Vanderhaar, Gerard. *Christians and Nonviolence in the Nuclear Age.* Mystic, Conn.: Twenty-Third Pub., 1982.

Vanier, Jean. *Community and Growth.* New York: Paulist, 1979.

Wallis, Jim. *Agenda for Biblical People.* San Francisco: Harper and Row, 1984.

———. *The Call to Conversion.* San Francisco: Harper and Row, 1981.

———. *Revive Us Again: A Sojourner's Story.* Nashville: Abingdon, 1983.

——— (ed.). *Waging Peace.* San Francisco: Harper and Row, 1982.

Yoder, John Howard. *Nevertheless.* Scottdale, Pa.: Herald, 1983.

———. *The Politics of Jesus.* Grand Rapids. Eerdmans, 1972.

———. *What Would You Do?* Scottdale, Pa.: Herald, 1983.

———. *When War Is Unjust.* Augsberg Press, 1983.

Zahn, Gordon. *In Solitary Witness: The Life and Death of Franz Jagerstatter.* 1960. Collegeville, MN. The Liturgical Press, 1964.